CREATED
EQUAL

CREATED
EQUAL

Why Gay Rights Matter to America

MICHAEL NAVA & ROBERT DAWIDOFF

St. Martin's Press
New York

For Don Romesburg,
for what is and what will be

For Martin Rochlin and Charles Myers

Design by Sara Stemen

Library of Congress Cataloging-in-Publication Data

Nava, Michael.
    Created equal : why gay rights matter to America /
Michael Nava and Robert Dawidoff.
        p.   cm.
    ISBN 0-312-10443-X
    1. Gays—United States.   2. Gays—Civil rights—
United States.
    I. Dawidoff, Robert.   II. Title.
HQ76.8.U5N38   1994
305.9'0664—dc20   93-44903
                                                         CIP

First Edition: April 1994
10   9   8   7   6   5   4   3   2   1

Acknowledgments

We wish to thank the people who encouraged us in the writing of this book, among them our agent, Charlotte Sheedy; our editor, Michael Denneny and his associates Keith Kahla and John Clark; and our friend Richard Rouliard.

Don Romesburg, Daniel Barth Peters, and Emilie Stoltzfus gave valuable editorial and research assistance; Sandra Campbell and Joel Smith helped prepare the manuscript. Many friends and colleagues read or listened to parts of this book, and we acknowledge their collective contributions gratefully.

We are grateful to the thousands of gay men and lesbians and their straight friends and supporters who demonstrated in the streets of Los Angeles in the autumn of 1991 and from whom we took—and take—our inspiration.

Contents

Preface: "Thank You, Rosa Parks"   ix

Chapter One: The Ick Factor:
Homosexuality, Citizenship,
and the Constitution   1

Chapter Two: Big Lies, Hard Truths   29

Chapter Three: How Prejudice Works   58

Chapter Four: "God Hates Fags"   75

Chapter Five: The Ghost in the Machine   113

Chapter Six: What Do They Want,
Anyway?   135

Conclusion: Created Equal   159

Notes: 168

The only freedom which deserves the name is that of pursuing our own good in our own way, so long as we do not attempt to deprive others of theirs, or impede their efforts to obtain it.

JOHN STUART MILL

This is your home, my friend, do not be driven from it; great men have done great things here, and will again, and we can make America what America must become.

JAMES BALDWIN

Preface

"Thank you, Rosa Parks"

1.

IN LATE SEPTEMBER 1991, Pete Wilson, the Republican Governor of California, who had publicly solicited the support of gay and lesbian voters, vetoed a bill that would have prohibited discrimination in employment on the basis of sexual orientation, a bill that Wilson had promised his gay supporters he would sign. In an apparent attempt to minimize hostile reaction to his veto, Wilson released the news on a Sunday afternoon. But word spread quickly through the gay and lesbian community across the state, and it was met with disbelief and fury. At nightfall, a spontaneous demonstration erupted on the streets of West Hollywood, home to many gay men and women. One of us recorded the incident in his diary:

> *Above the racket of passing cars, I hear the shrill noise of whistles, and then an echoing chant: "We're here. We're queer. Get used to it." By the time I reach the corner, the demonstrators have moved on. I see the flash of red and blue cop-car lights up ahead, and run toward them, catching the*

march as it slows in front of the two gyms on the north side of the street. The crowd chants, "Out of the gyms and into the streets!" And, amazingly, some heed the cry and we are joined by men in spandex shorts and tank tops as we move toward the center of the city, blocking traffic in the lanes behind us.

I look around. There are perhaps four hundred of us, a motley crowd that ranges from young activists in ACT UP and Queer Nation T-shirts to white-haired Morris Kight, who marched down Hollywood Boulevard twenty years ago in the first gay pride parade in Los Angeles. Up ahead I see Richard Rouilard, editor of The Advocate, *and Robert Dawidoff, a professor of history at the Claremont Graduate School. Fair-skinned Robert is flushed with excitement, while Richard is tense with rage. These two emotions, excitement and fury, carry the crowd forward into the warm autumn night. At the intersection of Santa Monica and San Vicente Boulevard we stop. For a moment it seems that no one knows what to do, and then people beginning sitting down in the street. Soon we are all sitting, while the sheriffs move at the edge of the crowd, trying to get us back on our feet. Someone begins to chant "Our streets, our streets," and it passes through the crowd, until we are all shouting at the grim-faced sheriffs at the top of our lungs, "Our streets, our streets, our streets."*

The demonstration went on long into the night, and in other cities across the state gays and lesbians also took to the streets. But in Los Angeles, the demonstrations were repeated night after night for more than two weeks, all across the city. As the demonstrations continued, they also grew in size until, some nights, more than five thousand gay men and women marched up to ten miles in a city where people are accustomed to driving to the corner supermarket. The demonstrations grew in purpose, too, from a mere protest against Pete Wilson's betrayal to an affirmation of the strength and unity of a community that hitherto was quiescent, if not apathetic. The two of us participated in many of those marches. For each of us, the striking feature of these demonstrations was how our fellow gays and lesbians perceived that their cause was in the great tradition of the civil rights movements of the past, a point made eloquently by a placard that read "Thank you, Rosa Parks."

The weeks of demonstrations culminated in a rally at the state capitol in Sacramento, where one of us had grown up. After the rally, there was another march.

> *By now it is night. There are a couple of thousand of us and we are marching back toward the Capitol. The quiet streets of my hometown are shaken by our chants. People come out of their houses to watch us pass, many waving or flashing peace signs, a gesture I have not seen since the last of the Vietnam Moratoriums in San Francisco twenty years ago. I don't know what we have accomplished collectively, but for me, to be back on these streets—where I was once a small, shamed boy— loudly proclaiming, "Gay rights now!" with hundreds of my brothers and sisters is victory enough.*

The emotional momentum of those demonstrations proved impossible to sustain over the long run, but they changed the lives of those men and women who participated in them. Certainly, they changed ours. Before we had been acquaintances, but after it was all over we were friends. And, since one of us is a lawyer and the other is a historian, it was inevitable that we would try to make sense of what had happened during those tumultuous weeks, and what it meant for the gay and lesbian community.

Out of those conversations came the basic arguments at the core of this book:

1. The purpose of American constitutional government is the protection of individual rights.
2. Gays and lesbians, as American citizens, are entitled to the exercise of those rights.
3. Demonstrably, they are denied free exercise of those rights.
4. The grounds given for denying gays and lesbians their rights are rooted in ignorance and bias.
5. The organized opponents of gay rights, who exploit this ignorance and bias, would substitute sectarian religious morality in place of constitutional guarantees that allow individuals to determine how best to live their lives.
6. These forces are using the issue of gay rights as a test case in order to promote a broader agenda, the purpose of which is to limit individuality itself.

It is our intention in writing this book to address these arguments to the great majority of our fellow Americans, who, we believe, would support the cause of gay rights if they understood that we are not seeking special privileges but the ordinary rights that all Americans enjoy.

It's worth saying now what we believe about homosexuality: It is neither a sickness nor a sin, but the natural sexual predisposition of a minority of human beings. This was not the belief that either of us had when he first acknowledged that he was homosexual. Like most gay men and women, we have had to overcome what society teaches everyone about homosexuality: that it is unnatural, a sign of stunted emotional maturity, a lack of self-control, a furtive and disgusting form of sexual activity without any affectional content; and that homosexuals are sexual predators and incapable of establishing lasting, loving relationships. We have had to examine these beliefs and equally pejorative others and test them against the evidence of our self-knowledge. For each of us, one in his thirties, the other in his forties, that examination was a slow, torturous process, because when we were growing up there was no alternative understanding of homosexuality that might have supported a positive homosexual identity. What we had to do, by process of elimination, was to come to the point where we realized that the cultural stereotypes of homosexuality did not describe our lives, our loves, or our aspirations. We discovered we were, after all, loving, decent, and productive human beings and that these qualities were not only consistent with our homosexuality but could, in fact, be expressed through it. For both of us, the process of self-understanding and self-acceptance took years, as it does for most gays and lesbians.

What we then discovered is that it is not enough to come to a purely private reconciliation with being homosexual. In our culture, the division between private lives and public lives is neither self-evident nor clearly demarcated. Law, custom, and public policy promote specific models of acceptable private life by rewarding some forms of relationships between people and punishing others. The institution of marriage, with all its social and economic benefits, encourages and rewards heterosexual unions, while sodomy laws discourage and punish homosexual ones. Understanding that government is not neutral in the sphere of private sexuality, we came to question its preference for heterosexuality to the exclusion of homosexuality, in light of our personal experience and our understanding of constitutional principles of privacy and equal protection of the law. The doctrine of privacy suggests that a major component of personal freedom is the right of people to live their lives without fear of unwarranted governmental intrusion. Equal protection requires that distinctions causing unequal treatment of citizens must be justified by something more than a prevailing prejudice against an unpopular social minority. Even before the demonstrations sparked by the veto of the antidiscrimination law, we had begun to think about our status not "as homosexuals" but as American citizens to whom constitutional principle seemingly guarantees the exercise of individual liberty.

When we began to think about writing this book, we looked for models that might guide us in the understanding of our task. We found such a model in the work of John Stuart Mill. When Mill published his classic essay "The Subjection of Women" in 1869, he knew he was taking on a daunting task. The aim of his essay was to counter the centuries-old pattern of male domination, to subvert one of the fundamental organizing principles of society. He chose the weapon of reasoned argument, knowing full well that the opinions he exposed were the bulwark of the prejudice he opposed. He also knew how limited the uses of reason might prove against ingrained belief, founded in feeling, supported by religion and custom, and reaffirmed by the rituals of individual and common life. He stated the object of his essay with admirable clarity: "That the principle which regulates the existing social relations between the two sexes—the legal subordination of one sex to the other—is wrong in itself and now one of the chief hindrances to human improvement and that it ought to be replaced by a principle of perfect equality, admitting no power or privilege on one side, nor disability on the other." With equal clarity, he stated the greatest obstacle to his cause. He recognized that the inequality he was attacking was supported by feelings more than arguments. Confident of his arguments though he was, Mill understood how resistant feelings might prove.[1]

Writing this book about the subjection of gay and lesbian Americans, we have had to confront, as Mill did, the realization that the reasoned arguments we put forward may not speak to the feelings that make people unwilling to support human and civil equality for gay men and women. As Mill wrote: "So long as an opinion is strongly rooted in feelings, it gains rather than loses stability by having a preponderating weight of argument against it. For if it were accepted as a result of argument, the refutation of the argument might shake the solidity of the conviction; but when it rests solely on feeling, the worse it fares in argumentative contest, the more persuaded its adherents are that their feeling must have some deeper ground, which the arguments do not reach; and while that feeling remains, it is always throwing up fresh entrenchments to repair any breach made in the old."[2]

A striking feature of the opposition to gay rights is its resounding restatement of just this "deeper ground" Mill identifies. Anti–gay rights arguments call on anti-homosexual feelings, summoning claims about the natural or the moral, the traditional or the proper, to meet arguments based on law, equity, science, statistics, and reason. Hoping, as we do, that our arguments for gay and lesbian equality make sense, we do not expect arguments drawn from law, history, social science, and personal experience by themselves to address the feelings that keep people from acknowledging democratic and human community with their gay and lesbian fellow Americans. We have had too much experience of those feelings to think that even our best arguments will do away with them. Like Mill, however, we know that such arguments must be made, and with Mill, we expect many of our fellow citizens to be prepared to think about them.

The problem of deep-seated anti-gay feelings remains. So, in addition to Mill, we have looked to another of liberty's heroes, James Baldwin. In his great essays on racial inequality, Baldwin summoned feelings as well as arguments to make his readers experience what the systematic subjection of black by white meant in individual and collective terms, as well as by the lights of reason and abstract justice. Baldwin's caution to his nephew that "you were born into a society which spelled out with brutal clarity, and in as many ways as possible, that you were a worthless human being," was also intended to shock his white readers into self-examination of the feelings and habits that sustained racial prejudice. When Baldwin characterized those readers it was to acknowledge how deeply ingrained their prejudice was: Whites "have had to believe for many years, and for innumerable reasons that black men are inferior to white men. Many of them, indeed, know better, but, as you will discover, people find it very difficult to act on what they know. . . . The danger, in the minds of most white Americans, is the loss of their identity. . . . Any upheaval in the universe is terrifying because it so profoundly attacks one's sense of one's own reality. Well, the black man has functioned in the white man's world as a fixed star, as an immovable pillar: and as he moves out of his place, heaven and earth are shaken to their foundations."[3]

We recognize that these same fears of shaken reality and loss of identity fuel much of anti-gay feeling. But, like Baldwin, we hope to dramatize the situation of gay men and lesbians just enough to challenge the hearts as well as the minds of our readers. If we can make the situation of homosexual Americans clearer, we might engage the feelings as well as the reason of our fellow citizens since, as Mill and Baldwin understood, arguments must engage feelings for change to occur.

to police because, as another study concludes, 14 percent of the victims feared more harm from the police. In 1991, anti-gay harassment and violence increased 31 percent in five major cities, including New York, San Francisco, Chicago, Boston, and Minneapolis–St. Paul. A 1993 study found that 28 percent of lesbians and gay men surveyed were subject to anti-gay harassment or gay-bashed within a one-year period, the vast majority not reporting the incidents to authorities. Yet, despite such evidence of the sometimes lethal effects of hatred of lesbians and gay men, the anti-gay right continues to object even to classifying attacks on homosexuals as hate crimes.[1]

Our point in this book is to expose these phenomena for what they are and to question their status. What is the argument for denying civil rights on the basis of sexual orientation? Is the "moral" claim of opponents of gay rights based on something the Constitution protects? Historically, lesbians and gay men have been intimidated into aquiesence in their oppression. One can define being in the closet as what you have to think of yourself to put up with the denial of your civil rights. But once you stop internalizing the message of inferiority conveyed by this deprivation and begin to see the second-class citizenship of lesbians and gay men for what it is, a whole spectrum of opportunity opens up. This is the source of the powerful contemporary movement for gay civil equality. This movement has replaced gay acquiesence with the demand for equal citizenship and has decisively shifted the constitutional and moral ground to lesbian and gay claims for equality under the law.

At times, the controversy surrounding the recognition of sexual orientation as a category of individual liberty makes it seem that what homosexual Americans are claiming differs in some fundamental way from what other groups of individuals have claimed in their movements for the recognition of their civil rights. Frequently, for instance, when gays talk about gay

The Ick Factor

Homosexuality, Citizenship, and the Constitution

1. A QUESTION OF TASTE

Homosexuality dis-
qualifies an American for citizenship. Whatever rights someone may enjoy on account of other identities, attributes,
accomplishments, and positions cannot ensure either the
free exercise of individual liberty or equal protection of the
laws if that person is known to be lesbian or gay. American
society still automatically accepts homosexuality as a sufficient cause for deprivation of normal civil rights, and American culture promotes the prejudice that sustains this
second-class citizenship. For instance, in September of 1993
a Virginia judge took a child away from his mother solely
because she was a lesbian. Routinely exposed to official persecution, common violence, prejudicial treatment, and denied legal recourse, gay and lesbian Americans are only
whimsically protected in life, liberty, and property, let alone
the myriad understandings of happiness.

Consider what amounts to a national epidemic of gay-
bashing. A 1987 Justice Department study reported that gays
are the "most frequent victims" of hate crimes. More telling
is the fact that 73 percent of these attacks were not reported

rights, heterosexuals hear talk about sex, not personal freedom. The claim that gays want "special rights" reflects the degree to which lesbians and gay men are seen as so out of the ordinary that their claims to ordinary rights seem special.

But in fact, gays want an end to their special status, their status as pariahs under the Constitution. In twenty-three states sodomy statutes criminalize certain sexual practices—specifically, oral and anal sex—that both homosexuals and heterosexuals engage in. In the 1986 decision *Bowers v. Hardwick,* the Supreme Court held, in effect, that these laws are valid when applied to homosexuals but not when applied to heterosexuals. It doesn't take a legal scholar to ask how these laws, which govern the most intimate behavior, can be an affront to the protected liberty interests of heterosexual people, and not also be an affront to the protected liberty of homosexual people? It was a question the Court declined, with startling animosity, to answer. Yet this refusal was itself an answer: The sexual behavior of homosexuals, the Court implied, is not constitutionally protected *because they are not heterosexuals,* even though the practices are identical.

Sodomy laws, however lax or intermittent their enforcement, are the foundation of discrimination, hindering family formation and preventing legalized same-sex marriage. They justify second-class citizenship and cannot be looked upon honestly without acknowledging that they still stigmatize certain citizens, making them virtual outlaws, and encourage and reinforce prejudice and violence against those citizens whether or not they break the law. Even in states without sodomy laws, the attitudes that support such laws persist, enforcing discrimination against gay and lesbian Americans in virtually every area of civil life. Seeking health care, employment, housing, access to public facilities, homosexuals encounter discrimination simply by identifying themselves as gay or lesbian.

A patriotic American who happens to be lesbian or gay

can only serve in the military by hiding the existence of a private life. The recent and thwarted attempt to lift the ban against gays and lesbians in the armed forces has not changed the message that has greeted returning homosexual soldiers in every American war: You can give your life for your country, but you can't live your life in your country. The line between private and public life overlaps for everybody, not just heterosexuals. The effort to compel gays to lie about their lives and deny their own human experience is itself a deprivation of liberty.

The constitutional status of homosexuals is inextricably bound up with the intense prejudice against them. The straight majority acquiesces in the constitutional disenfranchisement of the gay minority because lesbians and gays have sex with partners of the same sex and because that goes against the majority's grain. That, rather than any truth about homosexuals, has resulted in the common belief that gay rights are about sex. This struggle is not about sex. It is about privacy, individuality, and civil equality and the right of all Americans, not just gay and lesbian Americans, to be free. And, yes, that freedom must include the freedom to express one's own desire for sexual intimacy, homosexual or heterosexual.

The routine denial of civil rights to gays and lesbians reflects a powerful prejudice, one so pervasive and so connected to everything else in society that it is treacherously hard to isolate. Even when not activated into energetic hostility, this prejudice is deeply rooted in and continually reaffirmed by the rituals of family formation, child-rearing, and gender in our culture. One of the tragic ironies in the lives of lesbians and gay men is the degree to which they inevitably assimilate much of this prejudice against them. Another is how the prejudice against homosexual thrives, even among the family and friends of gay people. (But it is also true that people who know someone who is lesbian or gay are less likely to oppose gay rights than people who claim not to know someone gay; indeed, a recent survey of American voters showed that 53 percent of respondents who know someone gay are inclined to be more favorable to gay rights than the 47 percent who think they do not know someone gay.[2])

This bias against same-sex love has not been universal, nor is it founded on some universal truth. In our culture, because most people are heterosexual they regard the prospect of sexual relations with members of their own sex with ambivalent distaste. Prejudice arises against those who do not share this distaste. The prejudice is also fueled by the cultural tradition of encouraging same-sex bonding as a rehearsal for the eventual relations between the sexes. Boys and girls learn intimacy, comradeship, and sexuality from one another, the better to practice those things ultimately with their heterosexual partners; in this schema, homosexuality is perceived as a danger to maturation in the culture of heterosexuality. It presents an unwelcome alternative to traditional roles played by men and women in the formation of families, upon which the entire social order rests.

The decision to regard homosexuality as a species of alien behavior, and to punish it, makes a law of the majority's personal taste and habits. For most people, the "sin" of homosexuality is a question of taste. The question embarrasses people not because they can't imagine it, but because they can and do. The revulsion many men and women feel at the thought of sexual activity between people of their own sex remains a formidable obstacle on the path of gay rights. This revulsion, which we call the Ick Factor, equates distaste with immorality. It is a child's vision of life, in which the things one wants to do are natural, and the things one doesn't want to do are matters of morality: "I don't like it; it's bad." The undertone of the debate and the refusal to entertain a discussion about gay rights echoes the schoolyard din of "Ick,"

"Yuck," and "Gross." Teenagers apparently react this way to scenes of gay affection in movies. Of course, teenagers react that way to all but a few things. Adults are supposed to leave this stage when they assume the responsibilities and privileges of citizenship.

We believe that adults can think about issues of sexual orientation without being threatened as if they were adolescents imprisoned in the metabolism of puberty. We think that adults can learn to treat lesbians and gay men with the calm and neighborly regard democracy requires to survive. The prejudice against homosexuality is not so much religious as visceral, but neither religious nor visceral feelings justify the denial of constitutional rights in our system of government. Discrimination against gays reflects an awkward and inevitably failed attempt to isolate some people on account of whom they love, a matter that is supremely and constitutionally their own business.

Prejudice requires an elaborate social support to thrive, and the formidably articulated system of reinforcing prejudice toward homosexuality remains the bulwark of legal discrimination against gays and lesbians. What it all boils down to, however, is neither elaborate nor particularly complicated. At the core of the alleged "unnaturalness" of homosexuality is how unnatural it would feel to someone for whom it would indeed be unnatural. This distaste—understandable, though not constitutionally privileged—lurks among even those who wish gays and lesbians well and indeed would sympathize with, if not champion, their claiming of their rights. What blocks gay equality is prejudice. What fuels the movement for gay equality is the conviction that this prejudice is not constitutionally protected, but that the individual rights of homosexual Americans are.

Joined to this distaste is a corresponding desire to avoid thinking about homosexuality. Gays and lesbians have always been present in the culture, but when they have been acknowledged at all, they have been presented in stereotypic and restricted ways. More often, their presence goes unacknowledged, mirroring in the culture at large the determination of individual heterosexuals not to think about gay people. When they are forced to do so, the results have frequently been catastrophic for the lesbian or gay man concerned. Faced with homosexuality, family, religious, ethnic and racial solidarity commonly crumble; lesbian and gay people are likely to face ostracism from the very people and communities from which they had every reason to expect support. Every lesbian and gay man can recite a tale, frequently her or his own, about how a disclosure of homosexuality was met with revulsion, fury, and finally ostracism from parents, friends, teachers, clerics, employers, and the myriad others on whose support the gay person relied.

The dividing line between hetero- and homosexuality is a modern notion. Human sexuality seldom conforms to the explicit and precise demands of law and social policy. In societies as different from one another as fifth-century Greece and traditional Native American cultures there has been a place for same-sex love within and without marriage and the family. What is happening in contemporary American society is that people who prefer to be with members of their own sex no longer see this as a reason to be deprived of the rights to citizenship, family formation, and privacy.

2. WHAT'S AT STAKE

At stake in the movement for lesbian and gay equality are established constitutional protections of a species of individual liberty, called by the courts the right of privacy, and the more familiar guarantee of equal protection of the laws. The agitation for gay civil rights confronts the nation with the question of whether these rights will be subordinated to the religious and ideological views of a minority that blames gays and lesbians for what it dislikes and fears in society. Unquestionably, their attack on gays and lesbians amounts to an attack on individual freedom itself.

At its core, gay rights are an issue of individual liberty, the very individual liberty protected by the Constitution. At times, the controversy surrounding the recognition of sexual orientation as a category of individual liberty makes it appear that what homosexual Americans want differs in some fundamental way from what other groups of individuals have claimed in their movements for the recognition of their civil rights. Civil rights movements do differ according to the category of person whose rights are being vindicated and according to the challenge posed to whatever powerful interests are served by continuing the discrimination. Whatever the differences between the individuals whose rights are at stake and whatever the institutional and intellectual consequences of the movements, the ground of the claim remains essentially the same. The traditional American doctrine that governments are instituted for the purpose of protecting the fundamental rights of individuals, and the historical process by which these rights have been extended to groups who were enslaved, oppressed, and otherwise unacknowledged at the time of the founding, are the twin pillars of the gay rights movement—as they have been of every struggle to extend the promise of individual liberty to Americans.

There is nothing new in the opposition encountered by those attempting to extend to themselves the protections of constitutional rights. The fears that each historic new claim on individual liberty stir up are to be expected and remain irrelevant when considering the justice of the claim. In the process of owning their own rights, which is essential to free society, people unfortunately tend to see these rights as *exclusively* theirs and to view individual liberties as a limited commodity the extension of which will deplete their own store. On the contrary, the price you must pay for the enjoyment of your own liberty is the recognition that other people, especially people with whom you may not like to identify, have an equal claim to the same liberty. America requires an allegiance to a stern principle of individual liberty. This is the reason gay rights matter to Americans generally and not just to lesbians and gay men.

The character of American liberty is not static; the perfection of liberty is the metabolism of the American body politic. To stay that progress is to alter the fundamental process of our system. That is why the opponents of gay rights, like the opponents of every other historical struggle for civil rights, have to encroach on the liberty of the majority to prevent liberty from being extended to the minority. The movement against gay equality has already trespassed on the common rights of free expression: Witness the banning of gay books, the attempt to keep references to lesbians and gay men out of school curriculums, and the withdrawal by the National Endowment for the Arts of grants awarded to gay artists. This movement will go beyond present infringements against artists, teachers, newspapers, broadcasters, and publishers. Liberty, unlike nationality, cannot be safely restricted. Restriction turns liberty into privilege, and no American's freedom is safe if individual liberty changes from a right rooted in nature to a privilege rooted in custom.

In August of 1993, the commissioners of Cobb County, Georgia, passed legislation that declares the "gay lifestyle" incompatible with community standards. This unconstitutional nonsense was passed in response to two complaints about a production of Terrence McNally's play *Lips Together, Teeth Apart* in Marietta, Georgia. The playwright is gay and the play is set in a gay neighborhood, but the characters and "lifestyle" depicted are heterosexual. The play is about two heterosexual couples who spend a weekend at the house one character has inherited from her gay brother.

They learn about themselves and the state of their marriages. *Lips Together, Teeth Apart* is being staged throughout the country; its author is a major figure in contemporary American drama, whose plays are impossible to categorize according to sexual orientation. But, as this example illustrates, the restrictionist forces that have set their sights on eliminating lesbians and gays from American life and that oppose civil rights for homosexuals *must* infringe on the common rights to achieve their goals. There is no way they can restrict lesbians and gays without restricting everybody else: The county commissioners ended up cutting all county arts funding. Such guerrilla actions against classic American freedom show that what is at stake is not special rights for lesbians and gay men, but the basic protections that make American citizenship special.[3]

3. THE AMERICAN ROOTS OF GAY RIGHTS

Gay rights restates, as all great civil rights and liberties movements do, the essential grounds of American constitutional nationhood. Having said this much, we acknowledge that the extension of civil rights to homosexuals is a new application of the old American principle and therefore requires explanation. To the degree that it amounts to more than a venting of prejudice, opposition to gay rights represents the continuing efforts of those who mistrust individual freedom as the basis for a just society. The fear of individual freedom is an old fear, one that is neither mindless nor thoughtless. Most human societies have been founded on a suspicious view of individual human nature. The United States differs from most other nations in that its founders directed that suspicion principally toward the government rather than the governed, trusting freedom rather than power to bring out the best in people. They created a form of government that freed its citizens in a way that contradicted prevailing notions of politics and society in their day, and even in our own.

Reasoning from the turbulence, passion, and selfishness of human nature in history, eighteenth-century political wisdom concluded that strong restraints on all but an elite were required to maintain order. By contrast, the Constitution sided with democratic rule over republican restraint, and put its faith in individual, rational self-interest and passionate self-knowledge over religious, civil, and nationalistic orthodoxies. This confidence in individual freedom as the cornerstone for the best system of promoting the public good has always been the radical challenge of American constitutional government. In the Bill of Rights, the Founders denied the federal government precisely those traditional means by which allegiance, uniformity, and civil myth might be enforced.

The Bill of Rights offers an inconvenient reminder of how applecart-upsetting a system of government our federal constitution initiated. It is hard to think of a less convenient value for the legitimate needs and hopes of society than the notion of individual liberty, unless it be minority rights, both of which appear to be the object of the Bill's most interested concern. Effective government and patriotic community would be easier to achieve if the government could control what the Bill of Rights says it may not: belief; speech; privacy; independence of action; due process; local government; difference; uncooperativeness; stubbornness; ignorance; disagreement. The Bill of Rights presumptively charters everyone's individuality and self-realization. The enumerated protections amount to a defended space within which the individual and affinity group may thrive from the inside out, free from undue interference. The Bill emphasizes the point, made by the Declaration of Independence, that governments are the creatures of the governed.

One does not find in Jefferson or Madison a reference to

issues of sexual orientation. Historians believe that people of the same sex loved one another then as now. The defined categories of heterosexual and homosexual orientation were an invention of the late nineteenth century, however, and the open discussion of sexuality a development of our own time. The Founders did not think they were talking about sexuality when they were talking about individual natural rights. Of course, most of them worried that they might be taken to be talking about slavery, and certainly they did not understand themselves to be talking about women's equality. Like those raised by race and gender, the problems presented by being gay in a hostile society recapitulate the basic issues of the Bill of Rights. Among them is another standing inconvenience built into our system of government, which locates decision-making about how to live with the individual.

In our system it is the individual who makes moral choices as well as material, sexual, and political ones. While the individual's choices in these matters are not unmediated by the community, they are not to be dictated by it. The moral history of this nation might well be seen as the assumption by more and more individuals of their fundamental rights and their insistence on their part of the social contract. That we are used to thinking of these rights as belonging to classes comes from convenience and legal habit. But the equal protection of the law extends through classes to the individual, and the rights belong to the individual, not the class.

Freedom is the scariest of human desires. The American commitment to the freedom and equality of the autonomous individual has always frightened as many Americans as it exhilarated. For every Jefferson, there was a Hamilton who distrusted the unleashing of individual and democratic freedoms. John Randolph of Roanoke expressed the view of many when he said, "I love liberty, I hate equality." Then as now, fear of individual freedom was expressed in the impulse to limit and control it. To some groups, the apparent lack of moral order engendered by the elevation of individual rights gave rise to a persistent fear of conspiracy, the habit of seeing social unrest and change as part of a larger secret plan to destroy society. The "paranoid style in American politics," as Richard Hofstader called it, expressed this fear in the fantasy that secretly organized groups were gathering to destroy freedom—understood by the fearful as *their own* freedom, not that of their opponents. Masons, Mormons, slaves and free blacks, abolitionists, slaveholders, Catholics, Jews, immigrants, and Communists have all been viewed at one time or another as conspirators whose hidden machinations threatened the traditional values of their times. Not surprisingly, these fantasies share a fear of individual empowerment, a terror of human nature set free, and a concern that the marketplace of ideas was in danger of being overwhelmed by hostile ideologies. The proponents of these conspiracy theories characteristically suspect rationality as an instrument of politics and morality, because rationality fears fanaticism more than it fears compromise.

One curious twist in such thinking requires that the despised other be seen as superhuman, able to destroy great nations and betray the innocent. This thinking justifies oppression by turning its victims into predators against whom discrimination is no more than self-defense. Hence the need to fit the pariah group into a pattern of conspiracy and stereotyped immoral behavior, and to link these to an agenda that threatens everyone. It is a commonplace of democracy that the group fears the individual. One of the truths of our time is how that fear of individuality has become a feature of ordinary cultural life. What Alexis de Tocqueville called the "tyranny of the majority" regards with suspicion the individual who goes against the grain, choosing nature over convention as the basis of what one believes about one's self. The gay rights movement is but the latest in the long line of libertarian movements that have frightened those who fear freedom, and the arguments for gay and lesbian rights are as traditional as the fears they engender.[4]

As we have said, the movement for gay rights relies on two broad principles, the first is the individual right of homosexuals to enjoy the privacy that is the precondition for the enjoyment of civil liberty. The second is the enjoyment by homosexuals as a class or group of equal protection of the laws, which means essentially that one's individual right to equal treatment under the law may not be violated because one belongs to the class of people whose sexual orientation is toward members of the same sex. The individual right to privacy is a supreme constitutional value; equal protection of the laws is an inescapable constitutional guarantee. Without privacy and without equal protection of the laws, one simply does not enjoy American citizenship. The deprivation of privacy and equal protection constitutes the central ground for the gay civil rights movement.

When we talk about the right of privacy, we are talking, as the Supreme Court did in a recent abortion case, about a right that exists "at the heart of liberty," the right "to define one's own concept of existence, of meaning, of the universe and the mystery of human life. Beliefs about these matters could not define the attributes of personhood were they formed under the compulsion of the state."[5] Gays and lesbians do not constitute an identifiable minority along the lines of ethnic, racial, or class minorities. Being gay cuts across all human lines; gays and lesbians exist in all strata of society and in each group within those strata. For this reason, their struggle for equal rights particularly calls on the underlying constitutional principle of individual liberty.

In addition, not only the status of being gay but also the process of self-discovery is particularly individual. The lesbian and gay population consists of women and men who have arrived, by very different paths, at the same self-knowledge. The feelings that prompt ordinary people to love members of their own gender against the grain of convention, and the decision to honor those feelings, are different for every person. The decision to accept one's homosexuality occurs in that interior space where a person's deepest truths reside: the core of personal liberty. It is exactly that part of the self to which neither government nor other people's religion has legitimate access. This argument is not about sexual practices or particular lifestyles. It hinges on whether gay and lesbian Americans are entitled to the same enjoyment as their fellow citizens of the freedom to make choices about how to live their lives without suffering discrimination in consequence.

Heterosexual Americans do not have to think much about this fundamental ground of privacy because their privacy is already secure. In those instances where it is not, such as contraception, new law has been made to protect their privacy rights. The issues raised by reproductive freedom and sexuality have relevance to issues raised by gay rights; but, however important they are, they do not go to the fundamental ground of citizenship, as gay rights do. Privacy means that people make choices other people have to respect. The choice lesbians and gay men make to express their sexual orientation is quintessentially the kind of choice government has no business interfering with. That is exactly what privacy means, and this understanding of privacy is grounded in the natural-rights philosophy of our constitutional government. Such privacy is also exactly what homosexual Americans do not enjoy. Our private choices as individuals are not protected. As a group, we do not enjoy equal protection of the laws. The shared characteristics of sexual orientation routinely exclude us from full citizenship.

4. SEX, RACE, AND GAY RIGHTS

The gay and lesbian Americans' movement for civil equality raises constitutional principles as well as legal arguments, and it makes sense to consider the general problem of individual freedom in light of that movement. When we speak of equality under the law and of personal freedom, we are not—as even a majority of the Supreme Court appears to believe—talking about the right to have sex. People have always engaged in homosexual practices, with or without the sanction of family, church, and state. But sexual orientation goes beyond sex, because it involves not only the body but also the heart, mind, and soul. Sexual orientation involves the intimate associations—happily, including the sexual—that individuals form and that help give meaning and richness to life. The continuing categorical denial of basic civil rights to lesbian and gay Americans sends the message that their lives are less valuable than the lives of heterosexuals.

Sexual desire is natural. Sexual formation is social. To criminalize a kind of sexual desire, a society must articulate a common good that is rationally served by elevating some desires over others. It is possible, for instance, that a theocratic Christian fundamentalist state might criminalize homosexuality—along with adultery, nonmarital sexual relations of any sort, and all sexual practices but the missionary position—for reasons that make sense to its purpose as a regime dedicated to furthering its adherents' notions of divine revelation. The United States, however, is explicitly not such a regime, and it may not impose restrictions on individual freedom in order to serve the purposes of religious sects. The First Amendment protects religious freedom in the same way it protects individual freedom; such protection does not license the invasion of individual freedom even on God's business or permit the substitution of particular moralities for the individual, rational choices the Bill of Rights enshrines.

Criminalizing behavior is not sufficient to establish that a kind of behavior is in fact criminal. For example, intermarriage between whites and blacks was once criminalized in this country. Criminalizing such behavior served the recognized social purpose of racial hegemony, but it did not transform that behavior itself into something criminal, let alone unnatural. In a similar fashion, decriminalization of rape and violence directed by whites against blacks did not remove the criminal quality from such acts. The criminalization of the subject race in a racially defined society is an example of the kind of criminalization that homosexuals experience. To criminalize some people because their sexual orientation is in the minority is a crude tool of social policy—and, as it happens, that social policy serves no function in our society other than the preservation of a heterosexual privilege that does not appear to have had a beneficial effect on the social or moral common life.

Legal preference for heterosexual over homosexual orientation must be based on arguments about the human good in this society, not just on moralistic pronouncements. What reasons can be advanced for restricting individual sexual desire that apply to homosexual and not to heterosexual people? Stereotypical libels notwithstanding, gays do not commit sexual abuse more often than straights; the opposite is true, judging by rape statistics.[6] Family formation is not at risk because of gay and lesbian equality. In fact, if the goal of social policy is healthy family life, the equal recognition of families in which homosexual children and adults play a part will advance the purposes of those for whom strong families are the foundation of a good society. Lesbians and gay men do not prevent heterosexuals from forming families; and, as parents and children, lesbians and gays are equally capable of carrying on the social functions of families.

Being gay is what legal scholars call an "immutable characteristic," like race or gender. But sexual orientation is both like and unlike race, gender, and other characteristics that have been used to deny Americans individual rights and equal protection of the laws. What it has in common with other characteristics is that it is a difference commonly seen as disqualifying the different person from equal membership in the human and political community. Because some of the rhetoric of the gay rights movement uses the language and imagery of the African-American civil rights movement, it is worth pausing to consider the relation of the two movements. Race is, of course, different from sexual orientation. There are lesbians and gay men in every race, and homosexuals are as likely as heterosexuals to experience the xenophobia and share the material and political interests that give rise to racism.

It is often said that unlike African-Americans, gay people can hide their identity; like light-skinned blacks of an earlier era who "passed" for white, gays can "pass" for straight. This analogy does point out a difference: Gay people can hide. But the condition of hiding or passing is a surrender of freedom, of identity, and ultimately of life itself. Like the secret Jews of Inquisition Spain, and like those rare people of color who did pass for white, the unsuspected homosexual, trapped in an unwanted heterosexual lifestyle, pays the tribute of his or her own life to the system of oppression. Such a person courts dysfunction, misery, and shame without escaping intolerable oppression and special vulnerability to persecution.

There are, of course, significant differences between sexual orientation and race. The economic foundation and political establishment of the American polity can reasonably be described as having been founded on distinctions of race. The systematic destruction of Native peoples was enabled by racism as well as motivated by greed. Certainly people of color contributed decisively to the prosperity and security of a nation to whose elementary democratic benefits, not to mention riches, they were systematically denied access. Historians have shown how the extension of full citizenship to whites was coupled with the disenfranchisement of blacks. Homosexuals appear in all classes and so are as likely to have been part of the master and oppressor classes as of the slave and oppressed. Nor does homosexuality necessarily lead to the feelings of connection and solidarity produced by racial identity and class consciousness. Gays are sufficiently present in all places that their oppression does not automatically lead to a common politics based on identity.

It is worth noting that much of the opposition to gay rights among African-American and other racially and ethnically defined groups, including white supremacists, stems from less clearheaded arguments. The widespread influence of church groups on communities of color is as significant an element in perpetuating anti-gay feeling as it is in white communities. The groups in American politics that identify with increasing intensity with race are more likely than not to be related to particular religious dispensations as well; this applies not only to African-Americans but also to Latino, Jewish, and white-supremacist communities. The intensity of allegiance to church and the degree to which many churches minister to self-conscious and exclusive communities of race is a significant factor in the anti-gay prejudice that persists in race-based communities. Race purity and racial assertion also—especially in certain white-supremacist and Black Muslim sects—have led to the revival of race-based arguments against homosexuality.

There is another difficulty with granting gay rights parity with race as a civil rights cause. The African-American community has a historical identification with the civil rights movement that has led to a common feeling that the gay and lesbian movement—and other aspiring civil rights movements—are appropriating its rhetoric and moral claim in the same way that American culture has characteristically appropriated black people's other contributions, without including them in the rewards or credit. There is too much truth in this general assertion for it to be ignored, especially by claimants to the status of civil rights movements. To claim the mantle of such a movement—to invoke Martin Luther King and the drastic historical experience and heroic struggle of African-Americans, and to borrow their moral and constitutional claims—is a problematic enterprise. There is a particular historical character to the black experience, which no other group, with the possible exception of Native Americans, can simply attach. It is the paradigmatic experience of the deprivation and then the redemption of civil rights. It is hard to believe that any of the movements that have been inspired by African-Americans' struggle can replace that struggle as a defining center of what civil rights must mean.

But the special character of race within this society and of the civil rights movement that grew out of it cannot preempt other movements for civil rights. The black civil rights movement is historically unique, because the Constitution was explicitly amended to provide the freed slaves with a guarantee the purpose of which was to remove the inevitable burdens of slavery borne even by the slaves' descendants. Other movements took from the fight against this discrimination arguments and examples, heart and also a powerful metaphor, as they always had from the special struggle of African-Americans for freedom. "American ladies will not be slaves," declared the first women's movement.[7]

African-Americans are understandably sensitive and protective about the routine appropriation of their particular historical experience and particularly of the extraordinary movement they carried forward to challenge their oppression. Nevertheless, the movement's claim, as Dr. King repeatedly said, was to a common set of principles that must apply to everyone, not just to whites and not just to whites and blacks. If women, racially and ethnically diverse groups, and now homosexuals rush to the standard first carried by the African-American civil rights movement, that is not stealing but believing. Those who are so quick to denounce the appropriation of civil rights by movements based in gender, sexual orientation, physical ability, and various ethnicities probably need to examine their own record with respect to human differences other than race.

Although there are many grounds for identity and community among homosexuals—even across the important divide between lesbians and gay men—the deepest ground of sharing arises from a common oppression that has created a common culture and a shared form of desire that no doubt contributes to some common values. There is no reason to believe that the millions of lesbians and gay men in fact share connections analogous to the obvious and compelling ones of race, religion, gender, and nationality, or that even the groups that do share such connections founded in homosexuality are in the majority. The common experience of being gay is deeply individual. You discover your sexual identity yourself, your closet is your own, your coming out is individual.

It may be that the key contribution of the gay and lesbian movement to the history of civil rights and civil liberties is its re-emphasis on the individual. Being gay is an individuality that cuts across all the other identities around which civil rights movements have formed. It presents a challenge by individuality to group identity and group allegiance. The only culture we can say for certain that American homosexuals share is the common American culture. Central to this culture is a professed belief in individual freedom, yours as well as mine. The drama of the gay civil rights movement is less its statement of group aims than its necessary return to the ground of the individual asserting personal rights to personal freedom for personal choice about the personal life. The mandate of the common life is to protect the individual's enjoyment of this private life above all else.

The gay movement reminds Americans of the ways in which civil rights and civil liberties are not distinct categories and are not about the politics that advances them. It sometimes seems that "civil rights" has come to stand for minority group advancement and "civil liberties" has come to signify the rights of unpopular individuals. This effective division in the understanding of liberty is in practice a significant and troubling one. The gay movement refreshes the increasingly entrenched understandings of civil rights and civil liberties by requiring Americans of all attachments to recognize in their midst and in themselves a deep urge toward human expression and happiness and to acknowledge desire as a proper category of human life, integral to American liberty and occuring randomly within more conventional categories of identity. The gay movement reminds us of how unpredictable and how surprising and how individual rights can be and of why most countries have chosen to ignore rather than honor them.

The significance of the gay and lesbian movement for Americans of all sorts at this historical moment may indeed rest with the challenge that individual liberty is experiencing in this age of revived religious, nationalist, ethnic, and racial allegiances, in which the capacity to identify with individuals who are different is on the decline because the rational tools of that identification, and the critical self-examination it requires, are sadly out of fashion. Lesbians' and gays' claim to individual liberty and to equal protection of the laws coincides with a challenge not only to prevailing American convention, but to the communities that have regarded civil rights and civil liberties as their own possessions and not the responsibilities of all American citizens. How else, after all, could the situation of homosexual Americans with respect to basic civil protection be allowed to continue?

The black civil rights movement is not the only contested source for gay rights. The gay movement is as indebted to the women's movement as it is to the African-American civil rights movement, and its external and internal workings are alike defined by many issues that can be properly described as gender issues. Gay and lesbian rights raise questions about gender. We do not address those issues here, but do acknowledge that gender is probably as important as any other single factor in the resistance to the gay rights movement and to the particular character of the movement itself. Without the challenge to traditional understandings of gender and sex roles launched by the women's movement—a movement, significantly, propelled by lesbians—it should be emphasized, there would be no gay movement. The gay movement itself is unusual because its co-gender character is as significant an element of its purpose as the rights of the individual are. Because it is about lesbian women and gay men and because the history of that relation is so troubled and unfinished, the gay rights movement keeps questions of the sexes in the forefront as it seeks to reassert the province of privacy and equal protection for everybody.

5. HOW GAY RIGHTS RESTATES INDIVIDUAL RIGHTS

Lesbians and gay men who have come out and begun to insist that their lives and their choices about how to live deserve parity with the lives and choices of heterosexuals symbolize the fears of many Americans that freedom is going too far. For some, homosexuality is a marker of moral and social decay; the emergence of the lesbian and gay rights movement suggests to them not freedom but license. Moreover, among the religious right and self-styled cultural conservatives, lesbians and gays occupy the place once held by Jews and Communists in the practice of paranoid politics. Right-wing and restrictionist activists speak as darkly of the "homosexual agenda" as anti-Semites used to talk of *The Protocols of the Elders of Zion,* pretending knowledge of what they fear to know. Reactionary religionists warn of gays converting unsuspecting heterosexuals in the same way anticommunists used to warn of femmes fatales dispatched from Moscow to seduce innocent American boys. The scapegoating of gays and lesbians has less to do with homosexuality than with powerful cultural anxieties about family and sexuality, which express themselves in a wave of antiindividualist rhetoric.

For instance, a common argument marshaled against extending civil rights to gays and lesbians is that to do so would undermine the family. But in our system the individual, and not the heterosexual family, is the unit of citizenship. Families are encouraged, privileged, and protected in this system, but individual rights are not subordinate to particular definitions of the family. The "traditional values" argument against gays and lesbians amounts to such a subordination. It is an assertion that the nuclear, heterosexual family is constitutionally protected against the claims of individuals who form nontraditional families or no families at all. In any event, the family to which these moralists refer was the rhetorical invention of the 1950s; it was done in not by gays but by its own failures as an economic, parenting, emotional, mythic, and moral unit. Clearly, the "traditional values" argument has larger implications than simply as a justification for denying gays their rights.

The attack on gay rights also reflects anxieties about sex, a topic that both tantalizes and terrifies Americans. Gays and lesbians bring these subterranean currents to the surface because what distinguishes them from the majority involves sexuality. It is accurate to say that the gay movement represents sexual freedom—not "sexual license," but the freedom to live and act according to one's minority sexual orientation without fear of persecution from the majority.

The gay rights movement forces people to think about sexuality—their own and other people's—about what is natural versus what is normal, and about whether it makes any difference that some people are inclined one way and others are inclined another. The movement forces people not only to confront their prejudices but perhaps to face their own fantasies as well. The question of sexual orientation demands an exacting and, for many, extremely uncomfortable self-examination.

Gays and lesbians regard their position in the sexual fears and fantasies of their fellow Americans with irony and frustration. Homosexual Americans were raised by the same lights and with the same values as their heterosexual counterparts. These values inform their civil rights movement. The promise of individual freedom is the movement's inspiration and goal. Gays and lesbians experience that promise viscerally. Coming out represents a decision to transform one's life from the inside out, choosing the natural over the conventional at great personal cost. The same decision has been made by other people in other times, by men and women who acted out of self-knowledge rather than received wisdom, and altered thereby the political and social landscape. At one level, all the various civil rights movements represent the collective decision of individuals from groups of stigmatized Americans, who refuse any longer to regard themselves through the majority's eyes, and who therefore cease to accept the understanding that deprives them of their rights. Far from being a threat to their country, American gays see themselves in the American tradition by which such groups overcome their own fears and learn to assert their claims to liberty and equality.

The labeling of gays as sexually degenerate and unnatural is the same kind of labeling that has always been used to justify the denial of rights to individuals belonging to "minority" communities. It was less than forty years ago that a Virginia Supreme Court judge wrote in defense of the Old Dominion's miscegenation law: "[The] law which forbids their intermarriage and the social amalgamation which leads to the corruption of the races is as clearly divine as that which imparted to them their different natures."[8] Similarly, assertions of "natural law," warnings of corruption, and the invocation of the divine repeatedly find their way into arguments justifying discrimination against gays and lesbians. Such appeals are arguments against individual freedom because they deny the validity of personal experience when it is at odds with convention. Much of the fierce opposition to gay rights consists of this kind of denial. In effect, gay men and women are taught that their experience of themselves as decent, productive, loving humans is false, because homosexuality is unnatural and sinful. In this case, however, their own self-knowledge has helped gays and lesbians overcome the labels attached to their sexual natures. The process of coming out is harrowing, but it can leave in its wake an unshakable core of certainty of self.

Coming out is more than an acknowledgment, acceptance, or even announcement of one's sexual identity. It represents a continuing process founded on an act of compassion toward oneself—a compassion, alas, seldom shown by one's own family or friends, let alone society. That act is the acceptance of one's fundamental worth, including, and not despite, one's homosexuality, in the face of social condemnation and likely persecution. Coming out is the process through which one arrives at one's values the hard way, testing them against what one knows to be true about oneself. Gay men and lesbians must think about family, morality, nature, choice, freedom, and responsibility in ways most people never have to. Truly to come out, a gay person must become one of those human beings who, as psychiatrist Alice Miller writes, "want to be true to themselves. Rejection, ostracism, loss of love, and name calling will not fail to affect them; they will suffer as a result and they will dread them, but once they have their authentic self they will not want to lose it. And when they sense something is being demanded of them to which their whole being says no, they cannot do it. They simply cannot."[9]

It bears repeating that what is sought by gays and lesbians is not new or special rights, but, rather, the extension of existing rights guaranteed to all American citizens by the Constitution and identified by the Declaration of Independence as the purpose, not the gift, of government. Nor would the removal of legal disabilities suffered by gays and lesbians "promote" homosexuality, as is sometimes argued. Ending discrimination does no more than dismantle the props by which one group of citizens unfairly enjoys a superior status over another group of citizens.

We must also again emphasize that gays and lesbians do not seek the right to *be* homosexual. This "right" is not one within the authority of government to give. They are fighting for the right to secure the conditions under which they may lead ordinary, civilized lives. The argument for gay and lesbian equality is finally a conservative argument. America's character as a democracy depends in part for its survival upon the extension of equal protection to all citizens on the basis of a philosophy of natural rights.

Many people have lost their faith in natural rights and individualism. Identity politics based on ethnicity, gender, religion, class, or region is the order of the day. But the faith remains. Jefferson had it. It proposes that liberty is advanced by the wider access of all sorts of people to fundamental civil and human rights. In the world beyond the United States, we have witnessed the emergence of many peoples from the kinds of tyranny that most Americans have escaped or resisted. In the United States, the cause of liberty is often found in the strivings of its citizens from subtler, but no less pernicious, tyrannies.

The movement for gay rights would have surprised the Founders, many of whom, after all, were slaveholders, and who limited the franchise to male property owners. But they wrote a binding set of laws that were meant to surprise them. Their own habits and prejudices were among the conventions that the Constitution was meant to trump. They believed in the progress of liberty, which they based on their conception of human beings as rational creatures. The issue of gay rights is often lost in a morass of prejudice, religious and secular, but prejudice can be overcome by reason and reflection. We believe that when bias is put to one side, reason reveals that the cause of gay rights is a matter of simple justice.

TWO

Big Lies, Hard Truths

*A minority is only thought of as a minority when it constitutes some
kind of threat to the majority, real or imagined.*
CHRISTOPHER ISHERWOOD

1. WHY THE MAJORITY CULTURE STEREOTYPES
GAYS AND LESBIANS

THE MAJORITY CUL-
ture's attachment to its stereotypes of gay men and women
constitutes the single greatest impediment to gay and lesbian
civil rights. The anti-gay lobby exploits these stereotypes and
plays on the fear and distaste they call forth to justify the
prejudices that support punitive laws and discriminatory
practices against gay Americans. They could not use the stereotypes if they were not already in people's minds and in
the culture's folkways. To some degree, gays and lesbians
allow these stereotypes to go unchallenged, because they still
hide their sexual orientation out of fear or shame. Many,
perhaps most, gay men and lesbians still fit John D'Emilio's
description of homosexuals of the 1950s: "The dominant
view of homoeroticism as sin, sickness or crime accustomed
homosexuals to seeing their situation as a personal problem,
not as a cause of political action."[1] But in the decades since
the birth of the mass gay and lesbian rights movement following the Stonewall Riots, homosexuals have begun to challenge the prevailing stereotypes. They have come to see their

situation as essentially a political one and employed traditional political processes, from lobbying to civil disobedience,
to gain basic civil rights. They recognize how stereotypes,
misconceptions, and libels stand in the way of the recognition and protection of these equal rights.

Times have been changing for gay Americans. Despite the
secrecy that isolates and the specter of intimidation that
haunts the majority of homosexuals, gays and lesbians have
assumed a public and a political presence unimaginable
twenty-five years ago. Notwithstanding the strides their efforts have produced, there has been no outpouring of
support from their fellow citizens. Polling on the subject consistently shows that most Americans think that discrimination
on the basis of sexual orientation is wrong; up to 78 percent,
according to a *Newsweek* poll that asked if gays and lesbians
should enjoy the same access to job opportunities as heterosexuals. Public discourse about the rights of gay and lesbian
citizens, however, still responds to the well-orchestrated and
opulently financed campaign of the religious right and its
political allies who preach a message of hatred and intolerance that goes virtually unchallenged by anyone outside the
gay and lesbian community. The anti-gay lobby plays on the
uneasiness about homosexuality that the majority shares (as
do many gays and lesbians, after all) and which informs
stereotypic beliefs about gays and lesbians. The cultural tradition of stereotyping homosexuals perpetuates the uneasiness that keeps otherwise sensible people from recognizing
gay rights as the contemporary focus of the civil rights struggle, a movement for some people that restates and reaffirms
the meaning of equal protection and liberty for everyone.[2]

Stereotypes about African-Americans operated in the
same way throughout American history to keep white people
from identifying with black people and thus prevent them
from joining the struggle for civil rights. Similar stereotypes
dog the struggles of women, various ethnic groups, and the

disabled. The frustration and the challenge of a civil rights movement is having to explain to the majority things that people are not supposed to have to explain. It is tiring to have to keep answering libelous stereotype with reassuring explanation. Most infuriating is the fact that one must respond with arguments from reason and history, delivered in tones of conciliation, to views that are offensive and to opponents who have nothing but their own fears, prejudice, and secret agendas to offer. Why should people who hate homosexuals be believed when the question is granting lesbians and gay men basic constitutional rights and protections? No one listens to these people when it comes time to collect taxes from gay people or when they serve their country in the military or in the countless other ways that gay and lesbian Americans, like other Americans, routinely do. The challenge of democracy is that in order to claim one's rights, it may be necessary to fight for them. It is reasonable, if frustrating, that the majority of heterosexual Americans have been influenced by the tradition of anti-homosexual indoctrination that pervades the culture. Ironically, gays and lesbians have had to free themselves individually and collectively of the same stereotypes in order to come out and live their own lives.

Like the myths and stereotypes of race and gender, those about homosexuality reach far and wide throughout the culture. There are gay and lesbian activists and organizations working overtime to correct such libels, point by point, each time they appear. There is now a body of gay and lesbian writing, memoir, and scholarship on which to rely for this task. Some general views persist, however, views that support oppression, that arguments about rights must address. The majority in this country would never tolerate the discrimination that exists, did they not accept the stereotypes about homosexuals that sustain it. It is harder to tolerate discrimination against someone you can identify with than against someone different and threatening. This is supported by responses to a *U.S. News & World Report* poll, already cited, that indicated clearly that knowing lesbian or gay people directly increases a favorable view of gay rights.[3]

The reason so much time and money are spent by anti-gay groups to keep real gays and lesbians out of sight and to promulgate stereotypes is their realization that Americans ultimately will not tolerate institutionalized prejudice against other ordinary Americans. The anti-gay right realizes that for prejudice to persist the secret must be kept that most people do know gays and lesbians—in their families, neighborhoods, and workplaces—and hold them in esteem. You can continue to stifle gay rights, and the more general right of individual liberty for which gay rights stand, only if you enforce the cultural lies about homosexuality and homosexuals. That accounts for the astonishing energy with which the religious and cultural right produces new versions of the old lies. The depiction of the ordinariness of gays and lesbians and their lives terrifies and enrages the opponents of gay rights.

2. LESBIANS AND GAY MEN AS SEXUAL PREDATORS

The most commonly held beliefs about gays and lesbians concern sex; in particular, homosexuals are seen as sex obsessed, sexually compulsive, and sexually predatory. This view of homosexuality reduces sexual orientation to sexual practice. As a result, whenever men and women identity themselves as homosexual, their heterosexual listeners automatically think of sexual practices which most find repellent or threatening. Should you put a picture of your lover on your desk, where heterosexual colleagues put pictures of wives and husbands, you are taken to be making a sexual as opposed to a domestic statement. French writer Guy Hocquenghem observed that when a heterosexual man encounters a homosexual man a "spontaneous sexualization" occurs. The heterosexual, writes Hocquenghem, will ask himself about the homosexual, "Does he desire me?" As if "the homosexual never chose his object and any male were good enough for him." The controversy about gays in the military confirmed this view of homosexuality. For example, the chaplain of the Marine Corps issued distributed to senior officers a six-page memorandum in which he defended policy of discrimination against gays on the grounds that the military "believes for a number of sound reasons that persons with a homosexual orientation would experience serious difficulty in controlling their behavior" living in military quarters. Actor Scott Valentine (a heterosexual, incidentally) made this point more graphically: "When a straight guy meets a gay guy, right away he thinks to himself that the gay guy wants to suck his dick. I say, 'Doll, don't flatter yourself.' "[4]

This "sexualization" is applied to lesbians as well, as a North Dakota judge illustrated when he denied a lesbian mother custody of her son. Justice Van de Walle acknowledged that the mother's homosexuality "may indeed be something which is beyond her control," yet he claimed that forcing her to dissolve her relationship in order to retain custody of her child made sense because "parents in many, many instances have made sacrifices of varying degrees for their children." The mother's affectionate, stable relationship with another woman disqualified her from parenting her own child, because while heterosexuality denotes marriage, family, and social stability, homosexuality is completely and perversely eroticized and never the twain of homosexuality and family shall meet in the heterosexual imagination.[5]

The conflation of homosexuality with sex yields contradictory responses in the majority culture. On the one hand, gays and lesbians are associated with forbidden sexual pleasure and licentiousness, while on the other, they are demonized as sexual predators whose practices are unnatural and repellent. Gays and lesbians themselves, of course, have absorbed these attitudes toward homosexuality; as John D'Emilio writes, "A society hostile to homosexual expression shaped the contours of gay identity and the gay subculture."[6]

The charge that gays and lesbians are sexually obsessed takes a truth and distorts it. The process by which gay men and women are forced to think about their sexual orientation has everything to do with being a despised sexual minority and nothing to do with a generic sexual obsession. Heterosexuals do not have to figure out their own sexuality; the culture does it for them, relentlessly. The majority culture is obsessed with heterosexual orientation and its consequences within heterosexual lives. Heterosexuals are fish in the water, so accustomed to an environment that sustains them they never think about it; it's just "natural." So, "naturally," they assume everyone else is like them, that all men desire women, that all women desire men, that in fact the desire for members of the opposite sex is one of the qualities that defines men and women. The heterosexist understanding of sexual desire is an essential organizing principle of the culture; it is used to sell products and to explain behavior. In life and in art, romantic love between men and women is held up as the pivotal human experience for which everything else is but rehearsal or afterglow. It is not enough that heterosexuals experience this love, the culture appropriates love itself for heterosexuals as if the two things were synonymous.

Gays have to think across this convention for themselves. Each gay man and woman has to come to terms with his or her homosexuality; decide whether to accept it, deny it, or try to change it and face the consequences of the choice. Under these circumstances, it makes perfect sense that gays and lesbians are preoccupied with their sexual orientation in a way that heterosexuals aren't. The process of coming out, which lasts a lifetime, includes rejecting not only the culture's condemnation of homosexuality, but also homosexuality's reduction to sexual practices. As if that weren't enough, this hard-won minority sexual orientation becomes the distinction for which gays and lesbians are singled out and punished.

The association of gays and lesbians with particular acts of sexual immorality proceeds from the premise that homosexuality is immoral per se. Sexual practices of gays are condemned notwithstanding the fact that heterosexuals engage in the same practices. Gays are generically blamed for sexual excess and depravity. The religious right has been particularly vociferous in making the accusation of sexual immorality. When a fundamentalist group in Riverside, California, sought to qualify an initiative to repeal that city's antidiscrimination ordinance, it circulated a petition that claimed: "Many homosexuals practice oral-anal sex, group orgies, bonding, transvestitism, or sado-masochism or engage in fisting, rimming, bestiality, and ingesting urine or feces or gerbling [sic]." In their opinion finding the proposed initiative unconstitutional, the bemused justices of the California Court of Appeal observed: "It fails to make any distinctions between homosexuals based on actual conduct or deportment, tarring all homosexuals—male or female alike—with the same bizarre practices, gross promiscuity, and willful exposure to probable disease. It purports to solve the perceived problems by driving away the perceived perpetrators as a class, 'guilty' and 'innocent' alike. All that is lacking is a stone for throwing."[7]

Accusing all gays and lesbians of sexual immorality is precisely the point of these sexual libels. By characterizing gay sexual practices as extreme and repugnant, the anti-gay lobby attempts to defuse the natural sympathy that ordinary citizens might feel for fellow citizens who are, as a class, the object of punitive laws and irrational discrimination. Yet the same "repugnant" practices, particularly oral sex, are staples of heterosexual activity. It is unlikely that many heterosexuals would agree with Anita Bryant's description of cunnilingus as vampirism ("the tongue is used to stimulate the clitoris producing an orgasm is a form of vampirism or eating of blood"), which she intended as a condemnation of lesbian sexual activity: Heterosexuals engage in the very same practice. This particular equation of a homosexual sexual practice with psychological disorder was not original to Bryant. As the historian Lillian Faderman notes, "Some researchers of the early 1950s, who must have believed that cunnilingus was synonymous with the entire lesbian experience, and who misunderstood even that act, suggested that [female] homosexuality was really a manifestation of cannibalistic fantasies."[8]

Americans should be suspicious when charges of sexual impropriety are leveled against gays and lesbians in the political arena, because discrimination has always been justified by charges of this nature and because sexual conduct is an individual, not a group characteristic. Women, particularly, have been the objects of these charges. The traditional representation of women as virgins or whores reflected the expression of power relations in a patriarchal and sometimes misogynist regime in terms of a false generalization about women's sexuality. As the feminist writer Andrea Dworkin observes, "The [sexual] filth of women is a central conceit in culture."[9] The depictions of Anita Hill as a vengeful woman scorned, and of single professional women as psychotic harridans à la *Fatal Attraction,* illustrate how depictions of female sexuality become a weapon in efforts to deny women equal citizenship. Such accounts of women tell little about women, but lots about the men who wish to control them.

African-Americans, by way of another example, were not the sexual predators during the racial ancien régime in America. It was white masters who violated their slaves and who projected their own sexual compulsions onto blacks, establishing a racially coded system of sexual power. Thus the natural curiosity of black and white about each other was translated into sexual fantasies projected by the master class onto the slave, codified in taboos about interracial sex, and sustained by obsessive libels about African-American sexuality that grounded the stereotypes upon which the American racial regime depended.[10]

The allegedly uncontrollable sexual appetites of African-Americans, and particularly African-American men, have analogously provided a traditional justification for race discrimination and violence. As Barry Adam has noted, "Lynching was traditionally justified with the contention that 'many Negroes were literally wild beasts with uncontrollable sexual passions and criminal natures stamped by heredity.'" White anxiety about black sexuality was the subtext of miscegenation laws, some of which remained in effect until 1963. Jews have also been the targets of sexual slanders as a justification for anti-Semitism. Adam writes: "Excessive sexuality endures as a trait attributed to Jews by anti-Semites." Consider Hitler's description, in *Mein Kampf*, of a Jewish male: "For hours the black-haired Jew boy, diabolic joy in his face, waits in ambush for the unsuspecting girl whom he defiles with his blood and thus robs her from her people." Sexual innuendo and name-calling are, of course, a characteristic human form of attack against individuals and groups. Gays and lesbians are only the most recent group against which accusations of sexual excess are used to defend denial of basic civil and human rights. Echoing Hitler's charges of sexual theft, an Oregon fundamentalist group asserts: "The homosexual life-style is based on the recruitment and exploitation of vulnerable young males."[11]

The notion that gays are sexual predators is a projection of anti-homosexual sexual obsession. It is also fueled by the majority's refusal to recognize homosexuality as equally natural, if not as common, as heterosexuality and bisexuality. If one is unwilling to imagine how people of the same sex experience desire for each other or their consensual bonding, the notion that such relations are predatory must be invented to explain it. Thus, the assertion that gays "recruit" heterosexuals for homosexuality reflects an unthinking preference on the part of the majority. The notion of recruitment takes the place of feelings that are impermissible for heterosexuals to acknowledge and seduction replaces self-awareness and spontaneous desire, so gays become predators.

The heterosexual monopoly on socialization processes means also that anything that helps gay people be gay strikes the majority as recruiting, while the culturally defining barrage of recruitment of *everybody,* willy-nilly, to heterosexuality is not. If the non-gay reader of this book spent even a few hours experiencing the world as if she or he were gay or lesbian, this point would be instantly clear. Look, listen, read, experience, feel the cultural productions you encounter as if all the messages about heterosexuality were not normal for you, as if sharing a soft drink, buying jeans, driving a car, almost all TV and movies excluded your sexual orientation. You will realize just who is recruiting whom. You might begin to experience just how alienating and oppressive conventional life can be for homosexuals, and how ingenious gays and lesbians must be to fashion their own lives in so intrusive an environment. Our culture is in large part a majority-takes-all, reward-and-punishment system of sexual preference. It expresses itself by not only marginalizing minority preferences but by obsessively associating them with immorality and perversion.

Statistics on sexual crimes suggest no connection between sexual orientation and sexually predatory conduct. It is infuriating to have to repeat the lie to counter its dangerous influence when there is nothing to substantiate it but the sexual anxieties of some heterosexuals. If there is a class of sexual predators in this culture, as defined by statistics rather than hysteria and prejudice, it is heterosexual men, who remain most likely to indulge in sexually predatory conduct. This very fact explains the projection of predatory conduct onto homosexuals: It is a way of evading the crisis of male heterosexual conduct, evident not only in sexual crimes but also in child-abuse and spousal abuse statistics and in the incidence of children born out of wedlock and abandoned by their fathers. It is embarrassing to have to say that this unfounded libel is not grounds for denial of constitutional rights. Indeed, we believe that the gay rights movement is part of the solution to sexual exploitation, a problem that Americans are learning to identify, take seriously, and oppose vociferously.[12]

3. THE INVENTION OF THE HOMOSEXUAL

Another weapon in the arsenal of the anti-gay lobby is the claim that homosexuals are a tiny segment of the population and have nothing in common with the heterosexual majority. The release in 1993 of a study that revised Kinsey's figures to say that really only one percent of the population was homosexual was greeted with palpable jubilation on the part of anti-homosexual activists, who cherish the idea that there are very few lesbians and gay men. This, to them, establishes homosexuality's deviancy from nature, while at worst affirming its minority. The fraction of gays in the population is, of course, something that only legal protections for homosexuals and the elimination of the stigmas attached to being gay will reveal. It is already evident that enough Americans identify themselves as lesbian or gay to establish an alternative rather than a deviant presence in the population and that Americans who are gay share much with the heterosexual majority.

The notion of the "homosexual" per se is comparatively recent, an invention of the nineteenth century; the word was coined by a Hungarian doctor named Karl Maria Kertbeny, in 1869. In previous centuries, sexual activity between people of the same gender had been deemed a matter of taste or moral weakness, depending on the time and place. While this activity was often punished, in some cases by death, there was no sense of homosexuals as a class of people with whom society needed to concern itself. Not until the era of the Victorian "sexologists" was homosexual activity attributed to something other than fancy or the devil. As Michel Foucault observed: "The sodomite had been a temporary aberration; the homosexual was now a species." Some nineteenth-century sexologists rejected sodomy laws on the grounds that people should not be punished for what they had no control over. But the classification was not a neutral one; homosexuality was not just a phenomenon, it was a pathology. This view of homosexuality—congenital but pathological—laid the groundwork for homosexuality's subsequent psychiatrization—which, as Guy Hocquenghem observed, "has not taken the place of penal repression; rather, the two things have gone hand in hand." The medical model of homosexuality had one positive aspect, as Lillian Faderman writes, for those so labeled: "It was, in fact, much better to be a congenital invert than one who had the option of choosing heterosexuality and chose homosexuality out of free will. . . . For many, to claim a birth defect was preferable to admitting to willful perversity."[13]

But the far greater negative impact of the medical model was felt by generations of gays and lesbians, who were forced to undergo, or who submitted to, degrading and barbaric treatments the purpose of which was to "cure" the "sickness" of homosexuality. Jonathan Katz has unearthed documents dating to 1904, collected in *Gay American History*, describing such "cures," which ranged from castration to lobotomy and also included various kinds of aversion therapy. In one case history, grand mal seizures were chemically induced in a twenty-four-year-old lesbian. A gay man consented to castration to cure his homosexuality after the earlier "excision of the dorsales penis nerve" lamentably failed to "arrest the pervert eroticism [or] obliterate it." In another experimental treatment, men were given nausea-inducing drugs and then shown slides of naked men. "Approximately 5–10 minutes after the beginning of the session he feels unwell and begins to vomit as a result of the administered drugs." By midcentury, American culture had declared war on homosexuality as if it were an epidemic, with psychiatry leading the charge. In a jeremiad against the repeal of sodomy laws, a psychotherapist named Thomas Moore called homosexuality a "contagious moral disease" and a "menace . . . to the welfare of the state." Regarding a patient who asked "not to be cured of his homosexuality" but helped to accept it, Moore wrote he had refused because this "would be malpractice."[14]

The equation of homosexuality with sickness, and heterosexuality with health, persists in popular culture, which finds "evidence" of this equation in homosexual behavior without taking into account the psychological and moral effects on homosexual behavior of society's punitive and repressive treatment. Gay men, for instance, are characterized as sexually "promiscuous" (the term left undefined) and incapable of forming emotionally intimate unions, while gay unions are simultaneously derided as pathetic imitations of heterosexual marriage. Thus, in popular culture, gay men who are sexually active supply evidence of one kind of sickness, while gay men who enter into unions with each other supply evidence of another.

Similarly, the medical model of homosexuality leads to explanations of its "causes" that reinforce its characterization as a sickness. The authors of a sex manual called *Beyond the Male Myth* offer the conventional "diagnosis": "Men turn to other men for two main reasons. The first and most classical is the fear of the female, so that a man could not have intercourse if he tried. Such men have usually been raised by pathologically seductive mothers and rejecting or threatening fathers. . . . The second major reason is a fear of men, not women. The boy feels so inadequate that he dares not compete with other men for fear they will angrily destroy him." This unsubstantiated claim, replete with bastardized Freudianism, is an example of psychiatry as ideology rather than science, myth-making rather than observation. Until 1974, when the American Psychiatric Association removed homosexuality from its catalogue of mental illness, psychiatry played a long and dishonorable role in providing a basis for discrimination against gays and lesbians. Significantly, when homosexuality was still considered a diagnosis of mental illness, gay men and lesbians were not characterized as ill in terms of their own anxiety or distress but were "ill primarily in terms of society and of *conformity with the prevailing cultural milieu.*"[15]

Though deeply rooted, this cultural equation of homosexuality with sickness is demonstrably false. The world is not neatly divided into heterosexuals and homosexuals; sexual orientation is a continuum. The characterization of heterosexuality as normal and healthy and homosexuality as abnormal and sick ignores the diversity of human sexuality and renders a value judgment that, if defensible at all, cannot look to nature or natural science for confirmation. Alfred Kinsey's pioneering studies of human sexuality revealed that almost half of adult men and twenty-eight percent of adult women had had some adult homosexual experiences, ranging from the incidental to the exclusive. Kinsey summed up his findings when he wrote: "The world is not divided into sheep and goats. Not all things are black or white. It is a fundamental of taxonomy that nature rarely deals with discrete categories. Only the human mind invents categories and tries to force facts into separated pigeon-holes."[16] (We note the continuing controversy over Kinsey's statistics and their application to society at large, and acknowledge the claim that they may exaggerate the incidence of homosexuality in the population. We cite his estimates out of convention, until such time as a true account of the lesbian and gay population can be estimated. We also note that if, in fact, there are fewer homosexuals in America than the Kinsey study indicates, this underscores the urgency of protecting their human and civil rights.)

The gay and women's movements have in common not only the use against them of sexual libels, but also the use by their opponents of the "natural" and the "divine" as a justification for denial of rights. The argument that women occupy certain positions in society because of providence or "mother" nature was articulated by a nineteenth-century U.S. Supreme Court justice, but might just as well have been made today. In a case called *Bradwell v. Illinois*, the Court upheld an Illinois statute prohibiting women from practicing law. In a concurring opinion, Justice Bradley wrote that "the civil law, *as well as nature herself,* has always recognized a wide difference in the respective spheres and destinies of man and woman. Man is, or should be, woman's protector and defender. The natural and proper timidity which belongs to the female sex evidently unfits it for many of the occupations of civil life. The constitution of family organization, *which is founded in the divine ordinance, as well as in the nature of things, indicates the domestic sphere as that which properly belongs to the domains and functions of womanhood.*"[17] (Italics ours.)

As the recent controversy over sexual harassment in the military shows, these notions are alive and well. That controversy drew forth arguments about a "woman's place" (not in the military, and certainly not in combat) based on putative physical, emotional, and moral differences between all women and all men. The situation of gays and lesbians in the military has also been recently raised by the controversy over the military's ban on homosexuality. In that case, too, the argument against inclusion was based on stereotype: the notion that homosexuals are sexually wanton or would, by their very presence, have a "demoralizing" effect on their heterosexual counterparts. This view was expressed by the Republican Senator from Indiana, Dan Coats, who, while disclaiming prejudice, argued that the presence of gays in the military would make it impossible for commanders "to manage the sexual energy" of their troops.[18]

Coats, like others of his ilk, proceeds on the premise that gays cannot control their sexual impulses, something more likely to be true of United States Senators than of the average gay or lesbian soldier. Gays and lesbians are denied their rights because their heterosexual colleagues must be "protected" against them. If we did not have the historical example of African-Americans, it would be surprising to find a group of citizens blamed for its own civil disenfranchisement. The racist argument has always cast the disenfranchised African-American as predatory and dangerous. The imaginary "threat" that gays and lesbians pose to heterosexuals makes a lurid pretext for the continuing assaults against homosexuals' lives, liberty, and property.

The nature-based and religion-based arguments against gays and lesbians are even more vehement than those used against women. Implicit in the statement that homosexuality is an offense against nature is the premise that heterosexuality is a biological absolute, so that men and women who engage in homosexual practices are choosing to act against their natural sexuality. Therefore, the religious right asserts, homosexuality is merely a "lifestyle choice" undeserving of legal protections, which must be reserved for "true" minority groups, like the racial and ethnic minorities whose members possess immutable characteristics that set them apart from the majority. Race in this understanding is biologically determined, but homosexuality is not. The characterization of homosexuality as willful perversion is also a function of anxieties about the institutions of marriage and family. The right is looking for someone to blame for the apparent decline of the traditional family in which the father rules his subservient wife and children. Feminists offer one target, immigrants another, the poor (particularly the African-American poor) a third. But gays and lesbians offer the most promising target of all, because they can be attacked with impunity in a way that even women, immigrants, and poor people cannot, and because their very existence suggests how unrealistic and incomplete a picture of real family life that the "traditional" family represents.

The "lifestyle choice" argument, which views being lesbian or gay as within the power of a person's will to choose, ignores the historical evidence about homosexuality and the recent scientific research that suggests to many a genetic basis for homosexuality. But, more certainly, it flies in the face of human experience. There are numerous cases of homosexual men and women whom religion or pseudo-science have attempted to convert to heterosexuality without success. "Paradoxical as it may seem," wrote a Georgia doctor who, in the 1940s, induced convulsive shock in his gay patients, "every male homosexual I have ever talked with made the unequivocal statement that he had no desire to change his sexual habits and those who did were motivated by an attempt to escape the penalty exacted by society for homosexual patients." Or, as a onetime member of "Homosexuals Anonymous" wrote about fundamentalist conversion ministries: "There's no reality in it. I was selling a product, and my product was a lie." The lie is that gay men and women can choose not to be homosexual; attempts to stop being gay leave people spiritually and emotionally wounded, not to mention physically damaged, but no straighter. The most that can be expected is that they will be just that much more hesitant to venture their natural sexuality, which is really the point of such treatments.[19]

It would be a mistake, however, to condition legal protection of gays and lesbians on whether or not homosexuality is congenital or chosen. We emphatically have not tied our argument to whatever social or natural scientists conclude about the formation of sexual identity. The Constitution protects individuals and their choices. Moreover, even the supposedly immutable characteristics of race and ethnicity are as much creations of culture as of genetics. Racism, for example, is a consequence not of differences in human pigmentation but of how those differences are culturally perceived. Were pigmentation as neutral a factor as right- or left-handedness, then the concept of race itself would hardly loom so large in society. The unhappy truth is that perceived human differences, large and small, make a ground for xenophobia, fear, discrimination, and oppression. The history of left-handed children raised as righties in the many societies that regard left-handedness as *sinister* bears witness to the amazing capacity of human beings in societies to differentiate prejudicially on the basis of real or imagined, genetic, culturally formed, or intellectual traits. The Constitution stands in opposition to such irrational differentiation by extending equal protection of the laws to an ever-widening circle of people who, despite their differences, share a common citizenship.

The claim that homosexuality is unnatural is an ideological assertion grounded in religious opinion. Religious condemnation of homosexuality as "against nature" derives from the work of theologians, whose understanding of nature is not the result of a scientific attempt to understand the processes of the world. Rather, theologians construct the category of "the natural" as a way of authenticating their own views about proper human behavior. For example, the still influential Thomas Aquinas regarded all nonprocreative sex as unnatural. "The use of venereal acts [is] ordered to the survival of the race," he wrote in *Summa Theologica*; therefore, he argued, "the use of venereal acts can be without sin if they are performed in the proper manner and ordered to the preservation of the race." "The proper manner" excluded any sexual practice not incident to procreation, including masturbation, oral and anal sex, and homosexuality. Probably very few heterosexuals adopt Thomist views of sexual morality regarding their own sexual practices. Masturbation and oral sex, and to a lesser degree anal sex, are staples of heterosexuality. Although our culture has no trouble setting aside Aquinas's scruples when it comes to heterosexual practices, it sees no contradiction in condemning homosexuality as unnatural even though homosexual behavior involves the same sexual acts. As Barry Adam has observed, in the context of homosexuality "the term *natural* inoculates against reason or critical inquiry. . . . From the standpoint of 'natural order,' the social theorist can render inconvenient evidence into the ontological darkness of the 'unnatural,' the 'deviant,' and the 'pathological.' "[20]

Hand-in-hand with the assertion that homosexuality is unnatural is the belief that homosexuals are per se immoral. This immorality label is not only attached to gay and lesbian sexual practices but to gays and lesbians as human beings. Thus, a Republican candidate for the Presidency opposed civil rights for gay and lesbian citizens because "prejudice against [gays and lesbians] represents a normal and natural bias in favor of sound morality." Likewise, in the landmark antigay rights decision *Bowers v. Hardwick,* Justice Byron White equated homosexuality with "adultery, incest and other sexual crimes." The opponents of gay rights, a category that certainly includes Pat Buchanan and Byron White, can make this charge of immorality against gays and lesbians, not because it is true but because it coincides with generations of anti-gay prejudice.[21]

A chilling example of this prejudice involves Jeffrey Dahmer, the Milwaukee serial killer. Dahmer preyed on young gay men, luring them into his apartment, drugging them, murdering them, having sex with their corpses, and cannibalizing them. The local media characterized the murders as "homosexual overkill," a Milwaukee television station aired a series on gay cruising that gay activists believe led to the shooting of a gay man, and the mayor vetoed funding to the gay and lesbian pride parade. In effect, Milwaukee's gay and lesbian community, members of which were Dahmer's victims, was held accountable for Dahmer's crimes because many heterosexuals choose to believe that murder, necrophilia, and cannibalism are natural extensions of gay men's sexual practices. It is as if heterosexual men were held accountable for Ted Bundy's murders, or were to be judged by rape statistics and the incidence of spousal abuse by heterosexual men. (About which *The New York Times* reported: "American women have more to fear from the men they know and once loved than from any stranger on the street.") The Clarence Thomas confirmation hearings demonstrated how thin-skinned heterosexual men become when one of them is accused of sexual impropriety; consider Senator Alan Simpson's dismissal of Anita Hill's testimony as "this sexual harassment crap." Yet gay men and women are routinely accused of bizarre sexual excess, and these claims are then reported by the media, as in the Dahmer case, as if they were fact.[22]

Are there gay men and women who commit sexual crimes? Of course, just as there are heterosexuals who do. Are there homosexual child molesters? Yes, but there are many more heterosexual ones. Are there gays and lesbians who physically abuse their partners? Yes, just as heterosexual husbands and boyfriends beat their wives and girlfriends, and vice versa.

The issue of sexual standards, ethics, and appropriate behavior involves the entire culture, not just the gay and lesbian subculture, and to pretend otherwise is gross hypocrisy. To use sex crimes as a way of denying lesbians and gay men their constitutional rights is worse than hypocrisy, because it is part of a culture-wide denial of the realities of the abuse of human sexuality.

Unlike heterosexuals, lesbians and gay men must confront the problem of defining the role of their sexuality in their lives in a culture whose hostility to that sexuality is such that the only guidance available to them is self-loathing abstinence. Among gay men a debate goes on about the political and cultural meanings of gay sexual expression. While a writer like Michael Bronski argues that "promiscuity . . . is a way for gay men to reaffirm their social, political and sexual identities: the personal and the political inextricably bound together," his fellow writer Larry Kramer contends that promiscuity is the result of the denial to gay men of "every possible human dignity that the constitution was framed to provide us all. The right to marry. The right to own property jointly together without fear that the law will disinherit the surviving partner. . . . We decided to make a virtue out of the only thing [the heterosexual majority doesn't] have control over: our sexuality."[23] Promiscuity, monogamy, abstinence are common responses to the sexual drive among people of all sexual orientations. They are not relevant to the granting of constitutional rights, and very few people really think they are. Sexual libel is part of a strategy against gay Americans, as it has been a staple of every movement against extension of constitutional guarantees of liberty and equal protection to new groups of citizens.

4. CONSEQUENCES

A frequently articulated belief that contributes to the dis-enfranchisement of gays and lesbians is sometimes stated as "If homosexuality is natural, why are they so unhappy?" It is an attitude sometimes expressed by gays themselves, like the character in the 1960s play *The Boys in the Band* who said, "Show me a happy homosexual, and I'll show you a gay corpse." If by "happiness" one means a sense of security and well-being, the fact that gays and lesbians are persecuted, criminalized, denied their basic human and civil rights, and constantly threatened with physical violence gives them ample reason to be unhappy. Although there have been no studies documenting that gay and lesbian mental well-being is more precarious than that of heterosexuals, there is more than a grain of truth in the observation that gay and lesbian life is difficult by virtue of the social and legal pressures homosexuals face daily. The gay and lesbian subcultures, and some aspects of the social personalities of gays and lesbians, have been formed in reaction to entrenched and relentless anti-homosexual animus. This, rather than any quality of homosexuality itself, accounts for the sometimes anxious nature of gay and lesbian life.

Consider, for example, the very real threat of physical violence that gays and lesbians face even, and perhaps especially, in urban gay enclaves. In 1991 there was a 31 percent increase in harassment and violence directed at gays in five major cities: New York, San Francisco, Chicago, Boston, and Minneapolis–St. Paul. What kind of violence is involved? The *Los Angeles Times* reported in early January 1993 that a fifty-five-year-old gay man was attacked in the seaside community of Laguna Beach by an eighteen-year-old who was four inches taller and seventy-five pounds heavier than his victim. The *Times* reported: "Police said [the victim] was pushed down onto a rocky shelf of beach and his head was repeatedly stomped on. Hospital employees said the man's head was so swollen he is virtually unrecognizable." In a culture that seems to license violence against them, it is understandable that gays and lesbians feel tremendous anxiety in their daily lives.[24]

When a gay man is attacked on his way to his car from a gay bar, society seems far less interested in the violence against him than in its own lurid imaginings about what goes on in such bars. When, in 1992, the Vatican issued a statement that called discrimination against gays "not unjust" and seemed to suggest that if gays are the victims of violence it is because their agitation for basic rights invites violence, it expressed an attitude held by far too many Americans. In 1992 navy radioman Allen R. Schindler was killed by shipmates who stalked him and beat him to death, without provocation, because he was gay. The navy tried to cover the case up, especially its hate-crimes aspect. One of Schindler's killers, Charles E. Vins, gave evidence at the court-martial and received a four-month sentence. The other killer, Terry Helvey, got a life sentence. He told investigators that Schindler had not provoked the assault: "He admitted that he hated homosexuals and that he knew Mr. Schindler was homosexual. Mr. Helvey was also quoted as telling the investigator that he found homosexuality 'disgusting, sick, scary.' . . . Then he added, 'I regret that this incident happened and I feel like it could have been averted had homosexuals not been allowed in the military.' " Whatever else prompted his actions, Mr. Helvey reflected the libels and untruths society has manufactured to justify prejudice against gays and then, true to form, blamed gays for his own murderous assault.[25]

Psychological violence against homosexuals is just as pervasive and just as terrifying as the physical violence. Almost everyone remembers the high school "sissy" or "tomboy" who was the object of contempt and unwelcome attention from his or her classmates. Not all gay youths fit these stereo-types, but teens need only witness the disdain heaped upon those who do to be convinced that their homosexuality must remain a guilty secret. One result is, as we noted earlier, that one out of every three teen suicides is gay or lesbian. Not all gay teens kill themselves. In a well-known case in Southern California, a gay teenager's homosexuality was discovered by a classmate, who then exposed the gay teen to his father. The gay teen shot his classmate to death and is currently serving a fifteen-year-to-life sentence.[26]

We speak of gay and lesbian youth because all young gays and lesbians have experienced shame, despair, and feelings of worthlessness as a result of the culture's bleak teaching about homosexuality. As adults, many continue to view their homosexuality through the prism of these feelings. The culture creates a catch-22: It makes it difficult for gays and lesbians to lead contented, happy lives, because it oppresses them and then it cites the resulting anxiety and unhappiness as proof that homosexuality is pathological and should continue to be repressed. Novelist Christopher Isherwood said it best: "Do you think it makes people nasty to be loved? You know it doesn't! Then why should it make them nice to be loathed? While you're being persecuted, you hate what's happening to you, you hate the people who are making it happen; you're in a world of hate."[27] And all too frequently gay men and women direct that hatred and rage at themselves.

"Shame," writes psychologist Gershon Kaufman, "is the affect of inferiority" and "a wound made from the inside dividing us from ourselves."[28] It is also, in the case of homosexuality, a tool used to keep homosexuals subdued and oppressed. The shame that men and women attach to their homosexuality is not a consequence of their sexuality but of living in a culture that constantly exalts heterosexuality as the only "natural" form of sexual expression and correspondingly condemns homosexuality as "unnatural." Heterosexuality, it is understood, is more than a group of sexual practices; it is the cornerstone of civil life. The pleasure that parents feel when their teenage children manifest heterosexuality obviously amounts to more than satisfaction that their children will enjoy sexual relations with members of the opposite gender. It constitutes an acknowledgment that their children will become part of a community in which their sexual bonds are celebrated, legitimized, and rewarded as a ticket of entry and evidence of membership.

Heterosexuals pretend that all the dimensions that they attach to their own sexuality do not exist for homosexuals. Homosexuality is reduced to mere sexual acts. The possibility that two people of the same gender might create an emotionally fulfilling, life-enhancing union arising out of their sexual bond is ridiculed and obstructed at every turn by punitive laws and denial of equal protection. The existence of such unions despite obstacles is ignored. The fact is that most gay men and women lead, or try to lead, ordinary lives indistinguishable from those of their neighbors. They are the victims of sexual ideology in which, to be legitimated, sexual expression must serve the family, procreation, and the social order. Society and the law condemn sexual expression that does not serve these purposes as licentiousness. This ideology of either/or guarantees that the culture will veer between the poles of sexual permissiveness and sexual repression, and in either case, gay people will be held up as exhibit A.

This brings us to a discussion of a particularly effective weapon in the anti-gay lobby's arsenal against gay rights: the alleged "promiscuity" of gay men. The belief that all gay men are sexually rapacious is articulated not only by the religious right and its allies, as an argument against gay rights, but even by some gays themselves. For example, the authors of a book called *After the Ball* urge gay men to "clean up their acts" as a precondition to winning their rights. The myth of gay promiscuity is not only promoted by the Jerry Falwells of the world but by "friends" like Camille Paglia, whose obsession with gay male sexuality exceeds that of most gay men.[29] We do not join the routine condemnation of gay promiscuity to our argument for civil equality and individual freedom, because the Constitution does not condition its protections on whether a given citizen's sexual behavior conforms to the standards of his or her neighbors. (If it did, then not only some gay men and considerable numbers of heterosexual men and women, but also several recent presidents would have had their citizenship revoked.) In addition, we are not certain of what "gay promiscuity" means in a society where two gay men walking hand-in-hand down the street is cause for hysteria.

The allegation of promiscuity is less a response to gay men than it is a response to homosexuality generally; if many gay men see homosexuality primarily in terms of sex acts, virtually all heterosexuals see it exclusively in those terms. The heterosexual charge of promiscuity against gay men echoes with unexamined hypocrisy. In the majority culture it has been traditionally understood, and to a significant degree accepted, that young heterosexuals, and especially young heterosexual men, are allowed a period of what is euphemistically called sowing their wild oats. This is permitted because it is also understood that after a period of promiscuity young heterosexual men will become husbands and fathers. The difference between homosexual men and heterosexual ones is that gay men, after their period of promiscuity, are denied the alternative of marriage and family life, and are then blamed for their sexual conduct.

Young gay men are routinely denied healthy expression of their sexuality; as a result, they commonly exult in it, venture, and flaunt it when they come out—which can be at any chronological point of their lives. Finally, when the gay and lesbian community is visible at all in popular culture, it is noted not for its accomplishments in scholarship, the arts, psychology, or community-building, but for the sexuality of gay men and, to a lesser degree, lesbians. And even this emphasis on gay sexuality misses the point of the relation of private behavior to constitutional rights. We are not blind to the effects that the negative freedom of sexual acting-out has had on our subculture, and we worry about the effects on the ability of gay men to create other forms of intimacy with one another. But the behavior of some people in their legitimate private sphere is not a reason to deny the constitutional rights of an entire class of people who share the same sexual orientation.

There is no evidence that denying gay people their basic rights has any effect on controlling promiscuity. To the contrary, it is a historical fact that gay sex has gone on whatever the state of the laws, and that for many gay men such encounters have been their only chance for happiness, however fleeting. The Constitution takes no position on sexual practices—and neither should the law, except in cases of coercion and exploitation. The charge of promiscuity attributes to an entire class of people the activities of some and uses the attribution to deny the class its rights. If, in fact, the majority culture is concerned about controlling gay sexual expression, then it ought to legalize gay marriage. This would bring to bear on gays the same pressures and give gays the same incentives that it does heterosexuals to channel their sexual expression in a way that the culture perceives serves social order. Then, promiscuity, straight and gay, will be a germane topic of debate.

AIDS, a subject that we otherwise must leave to better informed members of our community, has had the effect of forcing gay men to examine their sexual expression. It has also led to the forging of closer links, and even community, between gay men and lesbians, who are often their caretakers, supporters, sisters. All this has altered the direction of the gay and lesbian rights movement, which now seeks to win for gays and lesbians, among other things, the right to marry and to create families. This is a different focus than was the case in the 1970s, when the mass movement first began to form. In the seventies, sexual permissiveness reigned among gay men—as it did in the culture at large, a fact conveniently forgotten by those who pretend dismay at gay male sexuality. For gay men, there was the additional factor that, prior to the emergence of a mass gay movement and the consequent shifts in perceptions of homosexuality, gay men were as likely to be sexually repressed as sexually active. This is because, for instance, police raids on gay bars, the only then-existing sites of community, eliminated bars for many gay men as a social and sexual meeting place.

Most gay men and most lesbians in the decades before the 1970s were condemned to lives of loneliness and isolation. Then, too, until 1974, when the American Psychiatric Association eliminated homosexuality from its catalogue of mental illnesses, there was no sense among homosexual men (except in the tiny homophile movement and the nascent gay liberation movement) that homosexuality was anything other than something to be overcome. In the 1970s, that perception changed, a change reflected in the defiant slogan "Gay is good." With the loosening of both cultural and internal restraints, many gay men went on a sexual holiday. Many gay male activists also perceived sexual activity as having an ideological purpose. What happened in the seventies was that, for the first time in American history, a generation of gay men emerged who could openly pursue sexual relations with other men without too great a fear of being thrown into jail or a mental institution.

Much of the gay male subculture still reflects the view that limitless sexual opportunity is the point of being gay. (Of course, potential sexual gratification is also used in the majority culture as the primary tool of advertising.) But gay men individually recognize that their political struggle is not about obtaining sexual partners, and that the perception that it is operates as an impediment to gaining their rights. As one gay lawyer said in an interview in *California Lawyer*, "It offends me when I hear [people say] 'I don't care who he sleeps with' at work. I don't care who people sleep with either. But that's not all there is to being gay."[30] We hope that this shift in perception about what it means to be gay or lesbian will also take root in the majority culture, but whether that happens or not, the rights of gay and lesbian Americans must be respected and guaranteed. Gay and lesbian sexuality, and the sexualization of gay and lesbian people by a hostile and uncomprehending majority culture, are both irrelevant to the justice of securing equal protection of the laws regardless of sexual orientation.

How Prejudice Works

1. PUTTING GAYS IN THEIR PLACE:
BOWERS V. HARDWICK

In 1986, THE SUPREME Court issued its controversial opinion in a case called *Bowers v. Hardwick. Bowers* involved a challenge to Georgia's sodomy law, under which Michael Hardwick, a gay man, had been arrested when his roommate allowed the police to enter his house to serve a traffic warrant. The police found Hardwick in bed with another man. Hardwick argued that the law violated his right of privacy. The federal Court of Appeals agreed with him, but then the Supreme Court reversed the lower appellate court. The *Bowers* opinion dramatically illustrates the vast disparity between gay Americans' theoretical rights as citizens and their actual position in society.[1]

Of course, a disparity has always prevailed between the universal principles of liberty and equality articulated in the founding documents, and the parochial, often xenophobic, practices of American democracy. It is for that reason that the courts exist as an institution on an equal footing with the political branches of government but are insulated from politics by the lifetime tenure of their officers, whose function is presumably larger than that of satisfying competing constituencies. The notion that the federal judiciary does more than decide the narrow controversies before it was introduced by the Supreme Court itself in the 1803 case of *Marbury v. Madison,* when Chief Justice John Marshall arrogated to the Court the duty of interpreting the Constitution. In recent times, the Court has come to be seen as society's conscience, before which the claims of individuals and unpopular minorities are supposed to be examined on their constitutional merits rather than through the prism of political expediency. Any failure by the Court to carry out its duty is, correspondingly, more than a politician's reneging on a campaign promise; it gives the stamp of constitutional legitimacy to an expedient decision. For that reason the *Hardwick* decision was particularly embittering to gay and lesbian Americans.

Michael Hardwick's assertion that the Georgia sodomy statute violated his privacy was a constitutional claim, not a vernacular one. In the words of Justice John Paul Stevens, the constitutional right of privacy "embodies the moral fact that a person belongs to himself and not others nor to society as a whole."[2] This is a different conception of privacy from that popularly used against gay rights; the anti–gay rights conception argues that if gays and lesbians kept their mouths shut about their homosexuality, no one would bother them. As Hardwick discovered when the police arrested him in his bedroom and threw him into jail, this popular notion of privacy is based on a false premise. Privacy in the vernacular, as it applies to gays and lesbians, is nothing more than a synonym for secrecy, but even if gays and lesbians are willing to keep their "secret," the majority culture is not. The charge often used to justify the repression of homosexuals is that this repression is simply a reaction to gays' "flaunting" their gayness. But as *Hardwick* illustrates, it is not the announcement of one's homosexuality that triggers the repression, but the simple fact of homosexuality. Homosexuality is a public issue, because the heterosexual majority has elected to single it out as a characteristic for which an individual may be denied basic civil and human rights.

Homosexuality, in this society, is the sole criterion by which the fitness of gays and lesbians is judged in virtually every aspect of civil life. A parent's homosexuality may determine whether or not he is given custody of his child, a soldier's homosexuality decides whether or not she will be allowed to serve her country, a job applicant's homosexuality determines whether that person gets a job or advances in a profession, a couple's homosexuality will bar them from marrying. The deprivation of these rights does not depend on whether a person announces his homosexuality or is discovered in his secret; homosexuality, not visibility, is the disqualifer. Therefore, when gays and lesbians are told that if they keep their private lives private—that is, secret—no harm will come to them, all but the most fearful recognize the bargain for the lie that it is, even if most heterosexuals do not.

What exists for most gays and lesbians in this country is a quasi-police state ironically like the one imagined by the anticommunist right of the 1950s. Those who grew up in that era remember the movies that were shown in grade school civics classes: Little Johnny woke up one day to find his Small Town, U.S.A., taken over by the sinister forces of totalitarianism, which were usually represented by a bearded, heavily accented commissar. Johnny soon discovered fear and paranoia running rampant through the town as children were encouraged to inform on their parents and familiar history was revised or erased. In the last reel, fortunately, Johnny woke up again, this time from what, it turned out, had been a bad dream. For gays and lesbians, however, the closet is not a bad dream, nor is the psychological murk in which many are compelled to live their lives. Gays and lesbians have no privacy, because even their closets have keyholes through which the hostile world insists on peering even as it sanctimoniously claims to be uninterested in what it sees there. If this analogy sounds extreme, remember that Michael Hardwick was arrested *in his own bedroom* for activities that by no stretch of the imagination could be deemed anything other than private.

The Eleventh Circuit Court of Appeals certainly had no doubt about the private nature of those activities: It ruled that the sodomy law was unconstitutional. In its opinion the court canvassed the Supreme Court's privacy decisions; it concluded that Hardwick, by "engag[ing] privately in sexual activity with another consenting adult," triggered protected rights of free association, and furthermore that such constitutionally protected rights were neither "limited to those with a procreative purpose" nor did they inhere in the marital relationship.[3]

The Eleventh Circuit's opinion was based on well-developed Supreme Court decisional law that stretched back for more than twenty-five years beginning with the 1965 decision in *Griswold v. Connecticut*. In *Griswold*, the Court struck down a law prohibiting the sale of contraceptives to married couples. It asked: "Would we allow the police to search the sacred precincts of marital bedrooms for telltale signs of the use of contraceptives? The very idea is repulsive to notions of privacy surrounding the marriage relationship." Despite this apparent focus on marriage, however, the Court soon indicated, in *Eisenstadt v. Baird*, that insofar as privacy involved decisions about sexual practices, it belonged to individuals *as individuals*, not in their roles as husband or wife. In *Eisenstadt*, the court struck down a law prohibiting the sale of contraceptives to unmarried heterosexuals: "If the right of privacy means anything, it is the right of the individual, married or single, to be free from unwarranted gov-

ernmental intrusion into matters so fundamentally affecting
a person's decision whether to bear or beget a child." This
line of reasoning led to the Court to its subsequent decision
in *Roe v. Wade,* in which it declared that the right of privacy
"is broad enough to encompass a woman's decision whether
or not to terminate her pregnancy."[4]

In its post-*Hardwick* abortion decision, 1992's *Casey v.
Planned Parenthood,* the court reaffirmed the central holding
in *Roe* and recapitulated the broad reach of the right of privacy. Referring to its earlier precedents, the Court said: "Our
law affords constitutional protection to personal decisions re-
lating to marriage, procreation, contraception, family relationships, child rearing, and education. . . . These matters,
involving the most intimate and personal choices a person
may make in a lifetime, choices central to personal dignity
and autonomy, are central to the liberty protected by the
Fourteenth Amendment." Moreover, the Court again rejected the argument that the right of privacy could be limited
by assertions of sectarian morality that advanced no rational
purpose: "Our obligation is to define the liberty of all, not
to mandate the morality of a few."[5]

Although the Eleventh Circuit did not have the benefit of
Casey when it decided *Hardwick, Casey* did no more than
state explicitly what was implicit in the Supreme Court's earlier privacy decisions: The constitutional right of privacy extends to individual choices that are "intimate and personal."
Gay and lesbian legal activists have long maintained that this
constitutional right of privacy not only protects gay and lesbian sexual expression but also creates a sphere of privacy
within which gays and lesbians may make other crucial life
choices, such as the cultivation of same-sex relationships,
without fear of governmental intrusion. The Eleventh Circuit's *Hardwick* opinion logically extended the Supreme
Court precedents to begin to create such a sphere of privacy

for gay Americans comparable to that enjoyed by heterosexuals. Before this process could evolve too far, however, the Supreme Court stepped in and cut it off at the pass.[6]

After Hardwick prevailed in the Eleventh Circuit, the state of Georgia appealed to the Supreme Court. In a five-to-four decision with a lead opinion by Justice Byron White, the Supreme Court reversed the Court of Appeals, reading its precedents as narrowly as possible in order to avoid extending the right of privacy to homosexuals. Contemptuously characterizing the issue before it as a matter of whether the Constitution protects "homosexual sodomy," White concluded that constitutional guarantees of liberty do not "extend a fundamental right to homosexuals to engage in acts of consensual sodomy." His proof? "Proscriptions against that conduct have ancient roots." The claim that such activity could implicate individual liberty was, he said, "at best, facetious." The Court, White added, should resist "discover[ing] new fundamental rights imbedded in the Due Process Clause"; he warned that the "Court is most vulnerable and comes nearest to illegitimacy when it deals with judge-made constitutional law having little or no cognizable roots in the language or design of the Constitution." Finally, White disingenuously dismissed Hardwick's claim that the law was invalid because it imposed upon him a morality which he did not share. "We do not agree," White sniffed, adding, "if all laws representing moral choices are to be invalidated under the Due Process Clause, the courts will be very busy indeed." In a short concurring opinion, Chief Justice Warren Burger justified the sodomy laws on the ground that "condemnation of those practices is firmly rooted in Judeao-Christian moral and ethical standards."[7]

If we compare the Court's rationales in *Hardwick* with its other privacy precedents, we find inconsistencies suggesting that what was really at work was a hostility to homosexuality that led the Court to evade both the implications of earlier privacy decisions and its own responsibility to interpret the Constitution.

The Scope of the Constitutionally Protected Privacy Right
Rejecting the Eleventh Circuit's extension of the privacy right to homosexuals, White attempted to narrow the right's focus to the specific controversies involving family, marriage, and procreation that were the occasions of the Court's earlier privacy decisions. But five years after *Hardwick*, in *Casey*, the Court echoed the Eleventh Circuit's expansive view of the privacy right. Referring to the due process clause, the Court in *Casey* spoke of "a promise [by] the Constitution that there is a realm of personal liberty which government may not enter. . . . At the heart of liberty is the right to define one's own concept of meaning, of the universe, and of the mystery of human life."[8]

The Antiquity of a Law as a Justification for Upholding It
In *Hardwick*, White justified sodomy laws in part because proscriptions against homosexuality have "ancient roots." Yet in *Roe*, the court dispatched an abortion law that was well over a hundred years old because it conflicted with a woman's right of privacy. As Justice Holmes once observed, "It is revolting to have no better reason for a rule of law than that it was laid down in the time of Henry IV. It is still more revolting if the grounds upon which it was laid down have vanished long since, and the rule simply persists from blind imitation of the past."[9]

The Role of the Court in Constitutional Interpretation
In *Hardwick*, White argued that the Court should resist expanding "the substantive reach" of the due process clause "particularly if it requires defining a category of rights deemed to be fundamental." In *Casey*, the Court reminded

itself that "our Constitution is a covenant running from the first generation of Americans to us and then to future generations. It is a coherent succession. Each generation must learn anew that the Constitution's written terms embody ideas and aspirations that must survive more ages than one. We accept our responsibility not to retreat from interpreting the full meaning of the covenant in light of all our precedents."[10]

Majoritarian Morality and Individual Liberty

White defended sodomy laws as a permissible exercise in moral judgment by the states. Chief Justice Burger went even further and supplied a basis for that moral judgment when he cited "Judeao-Christian" moral and ethical standards (as if his role were that of high priest, and not chief judge). In *Casey*, the Court responded to moral objections to abortion by saying: "Our obligation is to define the morality of all, not to mandate our own moral code."[11]

It is significant that *Hardwick*, the court's most restrictive privacy decision, was followed by *Casey*, one of its most expansive. The first case involved homosexuals claiming the right of privacy; the second, women. We are tempted to conclude that how the Court rules on privacy depends on whose ox is being gored. Evidently, the court has—momentarily, at least—abandoned its solicitude for unpopular minorities and does not recognize the constitutional principle that forbids Congress and the states from legislating on the basis of prejudice against such groups. The Court had abandoned this duty before: in *Dred Scott* and *Plessy v. Ferguson*, cases in which it upheld the slavery system and, later, racial segregation; in *Bradwell v. Illinois*, when it reinforced the culturally inferior position of women by upholding a law that barred them from practicing law; and in *Korematsu*, when it upheld the internment of Japanese-Americans.

It was the plaintiffs in these cases, rather than the majority of the Supreme Court, who were constitutionally in the right. Subsequent history has vindicated their actions and condemned the Court's refusal to defend their personal liberty and their right to equal protection of the law. It is the same with Michael Hardwick and his fellow gay and lesbian citizens. The right of privacy, that fundamental ground of everyone's daily life, coincides exactly with the choices gays and lesbians have to make when they come out of the closet to lead normal lives. The Constitution protects personal autonomy and even (perhaps especially) the unpopular decisions that people make to live authentic lives. The test for the morality of these lives is not whether they please other people, but whether they harm them, a point recently made by the Kentucky Supreme Court when it invalidated that state's sodomy law. Justice Dan Jack Combs's concurring opinion in that case reminded citizens "what a Constitution is and what it is not. It is an instrument by which the people created a government and invested it with certain powers, directed to a specific end. The Constitution does not create any rights of, or grant any rights to, the people. It merely recognizes their primordial rights, and constructs a government as a means of protecting and preserving them. . . . The purpose of the Government born of the Constitution is to protect these individual liberties, not take them away. . . . Ordained as the jealous guardian of individual freedom, government wields legitimate power only in the execution of that function. Its authority to interfere with one's liberty derives solely from its duty to preserve the liberty of another."[12]

It was precisely this analysis of whether the exercise of liberty by one individual infringes on the liberty of another that the Supreme Court avoided in *Hardwick*, for reasons all too apparent from its sensationalistic characterization of the issue before it (the right to "homosexual sodomy"). Instead, the Court relied on popular prejudice and religious belief. The point of the Bill of Rights, of course, is to protect individual liberty from popular opinion and religious belief, especially when these are enforced or tolerated by government action or inaction. In *Hardwick,* unhappily, the Supreme Court blunted this essential point of our constitutional regime. In his dissent, Justice Harry Blackmun, joined by three other justices, wrote: "I can only hope that . . . the Court will reconsider its analysis and conclude that depriving individuals of the right to choose for themselves how to conduct their intimate relationships poses a far greater threat to the values most deeply rooted in our Nation's history than tolerance of nonconformity could ever do. Because I think the court betrays those values, I dissent." Blackmun's point is also ours: Everyone's freedom suffers when individual liberty is denied to a class of citizens.[13]

2. CREATING THE "LAVENDER LINE": COLORADO'S AMENDMENT 2

On November 8, 1992, the people of Colorado made history when they enacted a state constitutional amendment that prohibited any governmental agency from adopting statutes or policies protecting gays from discrimination. Not since post-Reconstruction southern states created the system of racial apartheid popularly known as Jim Crow laws has a state so explicitly divided its citizens into two castes—one that enjoys all the rights and privileges of citizenship, and another systematically denied those rights.

Amendment 2 had other, more direct, precedents as well. Most notorious is the military's ban on openly gay and lesbian soldiers from serving in the armed forces. Less well known are certain sodomy laws, adopted by a handful of states, that are applicable *only* to homosexual sexual activity. In California, generally a progressive state for gay and lesbian rights, the legislature amended the marriage statute in the mid-seventies to define marriage as the union of a man and a woman; it did so with the specific intention of denying gays the right to marry. The legislation was signed into law by that supposed friend of the gay community, Jerry Brown. Except for the military ban, none of these laws had the sweep of Amendment 2, which not only prohibited antidiscrimination laws but repealed such laws as already existed in a handful of Colorado cities.

Amendment 2 represents the latest tactic in the religious right's ongoing war against gay and lesbian Americans. Unlike a similar proposal in Oregon that, among other things, required educators to set curriculum standards equating homosexuality with pedophilia, sadism, and masochism as behaviors to be avoided (and lost at the polls), the Colorado initiative was phrased in neutral and legalistic terms. It reads: "Neither the State of Colorado, through any of its branches or departments, nor any of its agencies, political subdivisions, municipalities or school districts, shall enact, adopt or enforce any statute, regulation, ordinance or policy whereby homosexual, lesbian, or bisexual orientation, conduct, practices or relationships shall constitute or otherwise be the basis of, or entitle any person or class of persons to have or claim any minority status, quota preferences, protected status or claim of discrimination."[14]

Although the effect of the amendment would have been and may yet be to legalize discrimination against gays and lesbians, the lack of overt bigotry in its language, and the insertion of the buzzwords "quota preferences," allowed its backers to maintain that the purpose of the law was simply to prevent homosexuals from enjoying "special rights." What Amendment 2 really attacked, however, was the Fourteenth Amendment's guarantee of equal protection of the laws.

As it has evolved in the context of modern civil rights movements, the equal protection clause has served to invalidate discriminatory practices based on arbitrary distinctions between individuals who are otherwise identically situated. A classic example: In the case of two potential voters, one black and one white, equal protection prohibits denying the franchise to the potential black voter because of his race. Equal protection is about fundamental fairness. State action that treats some people differently than others is examined by the courts to determine whether a legitimate justification exists for the unequal treatment. Where, moreover, the law singles out a "discrete and insular" minority, the classification is "suspect" and accorded "searching judicial inquiry."[15]

Simply stated, what equal protection has come to mean is that laws that single out and discriminate against a particular group of citizens must advance a legitimate purpose of the state and not simply codify popular prejudice against the targeted group. As articulated by the Ninth Circuit Court of Appeals in a case that reinstated a gay soldier to the military, under the equal protection doctrine "laws that limit the acceptable focus of one's sexual desires to members of the opposite sex, like laws that limit one's choice of spouse (or sexual partner) to members of the same race, cannot withstand constitutional scrutiny absent a compelling justification."[16]

The quest by gay Americans for equal protection of the laws has become the flash point in the ongoing debate over gay rights generally. Amendment 2 was a response to that struggle. When we were writing this book, the Colorado Supreme Court ruled on a lawsuit that had successfully enjoined the enforcement of Amendment 2 pending a trial on its constitutionality. The Supreme Court affirmed the injunction in an opinion based on an equal protection analysis. The plaintiffs argued that because of the difficulty of overturning a constitutional amendment, Amendment 2 violated their right to participate equally in the political process and therefore violated equal protection. The Colorado Supreme Court agreed that the "Equal Protection Clause guarantees the fundamental right to participate equally in the political process and thus, any attempt to infringe on that right must be subject to strict scrutiny and can be held constitutionally valid only if supported by a compelling state interest." The court characterized Amendment 2 as singling out "a class of people [namely gay men, lesbians, and bisexuals] who would benefit from laws barring discrimination on the basis of sexual orientation. No other identifiable group faces such a burden.... Such a structuring of the political process is contrary to the notion that 'the concept of we the people under the Constitution visualizes no preferred class of voters but equality among those who meet basic qualifications.'" The court held that although Amendment 2 had been passed by a majority of voters and therefore was entitled to "great deference": "The fact remains that 'one's life, liberty, and property ... and other fundamental rights may not be submitted to vote.'"[17]

The points made by the Colorado Supreme Court are precisely those that animate this book. The rights of American citizens are not dependent on whether those Americans are popular, but arise by virtue of their citizenship. Correspondingly, any attempt to restrict the free exercise of those rights because of a popular prejudice cannot withstand the searching scrutiny required by the courts and the equal protection clause.

The "special rights" rhetoric of the antigay right is really an attempt to draw a line—a lavender line—between "us" and "them." Typically, anti-discrimination laws do no more than prevent gays and lesbians from being fired from their jobs and denied housing or medical care because they are gay. These can be deemed "special rights" only if a job, food to eat, a place to live, and medical attention are unusual demands. Behind the cry of "No special rights" is an effort to protect heterosexual privilege in the culture by denying such privilege to homosexuals.[18]

By "heterosexual privilege" we mean all those rights and entitlements that heterosexuals enjoy in the construction of their private lives—including, for example, protected sexual expressiveness and marriage. It is indisputable that most people are heterosexual (or, at least, identify themselves as such). Our point is not to deny this nor to require that homosexuality be taught by the culture in the same way as heterosexuality is taught. What needs to be recognized and acknowledged, however, is that heterosexuality is not only taught but *enforced,* at great cost to those of us who are not and cannot be heterosexual. What we seek is a space in which to construct our own lives with the same opportunities that heterosexuals enjoy.

Understand, we do not expect that this society will ever enshrine homosexuality the way it does heterosexuality. But at the very least, society must shed its punitive attitudes toward homosexuality and encourage institutions and families that acknowledge it as the basis for a morally serious life. We say "morally serious," rather than "moral," for a reason. People live different moral lives; their freedom to make moral choices is constitutionally protected. What we want is a society in which gays and lesbians are as free to make these choices as heterosexuals. Heterosexual privilege removes the moral seriousness of gay lives because it strips those lives of their dignity; and dignity, like honor, is fundamental to moral seriousness.

The enormous pressure on homosexuals to pretend they are heterosexuals is ultimately destructive not merely of individual lives but of the life of the society as well. The legal gray zone in which gays and lesbians are forced to lead their lives is a constant affront to the democratic ideals upon which this country claims to be based. To drive a whole class of individuals underground and to punish them when they surface—individuals who cannot change who they are—is both arbitrary and cruel, and it creates a society that is arbitrary and cruel. The hypocrisy that closeted gays and lesbians adopt to conceal themselves cannot be blamed on them alone, but reflects a hypocritical and cynical society that intermittently acknowledges homosexuality but publicly disavows its legitimacy.

Heterosexual privilege and the social and belief system it structures fail to take into account the way most people live their lives today. Most people no longer live in a "traditional" family, and many gays and lesbians have tried to carve out some kind of family. These events can be deplored and punished or they can be acknowledged as the factual basis of genuinely pro-family policies, policies that support, among other people, gay families and gay children. Heterosexual privilege needs to be replaced with the privileging of families as they exist.

This is precisely what the proponents of measures like Amendment 2 are fighting against. They prefer a form of American society that is now obsolete, if it ever existed, and they think that the only way they can resurrect it is through ever more punitive laws that violate the basic principles of American constitutional democracy. The arguments they deploy against gays and lesbians illustrate the radical nature of their political ideology. For example, the anti-gay right asserts that homosexuality is merely a form of chosen conduct and that conduct is undeserving of civil rights protection. The same argument could be made about women who divorce their husbands: They have chosen to leave their marriages and, as a consequence, are undeserving of the custody of their children or their share of the marital property. Even assuming, for the sake of argument, that homosexuality is chosen conduct, that reason alone does not disqualify homosexuals from the equal protection of the laws. Whether a choice is protected depends on how intimately that choice is related to what the courts called "personhood," and on the potential that a person so choosing will, by that choice, encounter bias.

We believe homosexuality is not a choice but innate. Recent natural and social scientific inquiry supports our belief, but we do not rest it principally on that evidence. The clinching evidence is the testimony of lesbians and gay men themselves. Since the emergence of a mass gay rights movement, there have been thousands of books by gays and lesbians about their own lives and the lives of others. This body of work represents the testimony of those who have the most knowledge of homosexuality, and lesbians and gay men consistently speak of their homosexuality as something in their natures over which they exercise no control. Yet despite this evidence, the old justifications continue unabated; pseudoscience and sectarian morality extend personal distaste or fear into a claim about the natural, so as to support discrimination against gay Americans. In time, we believe, these rationalizations will fall, but this can happen only when a sufficient number of people are willing to look at the damage this discrimination has caused millions of lives and society as a whole.

Colorado's Amendment 2 and the other initiatives of a similar kind that opponents of gay rights are attempting to enact across the country bring into the public arena the experience lesbians and gay men have had to endure on their own. Difficult and enraging as these public moves against us are, they are the result of gay and lesbian self-assertion. To restrain us, the anti-homosexual activists have to show themselves and their arguments for what they are: ignorant, prejudiced, and in clear opposition to the guarantees of equal protection and individual liberty that are the hallmarks of our society. Anti-gay activists must reveal how their attempts to restrict the freedoms of lesbians and gay men lead to restricting the liberties of everybody. They must insist on controlling classroom and laboratory; they must either censor or defund public arts and cultural affairs; they must interfere with health and human services. As tyrants always do, they underestimate the willingness of people to stand up for freedom, and they underestimate the intelligence of Americans, who do understand why everyone's liberties matter to them. The lavender line—like the color line and the gender line and religious lines and class lines and ethnic lines—will fail, because as someone once observed, a house divided against itself cannot stand.[19]

FOUR

"God Hates Fags"

1. FUNDAMENTALISM AND THE
FUNDAMENTALS OF FREEDOM

IT WOULD BE EASY TO conclude that God does hate homosexuals—that is, if you paid attention to the routine homophobia of so many self-described religious authorities. Religion is regularly used to discourage homosexuals from coming out and leading their own lives, and God is invoked to justify the denial of equality to gays and lesbians. In the words of one religious pamphlet, "God hates homosexuality as much today as he did in Lot's day. . . . God sits in judgment on homosexuals. We are at liberty to inform them how God feels about the sexual scourge, as the apostle Paul did." The title of this chapter is another illustration of that sentiment; it quotes a placard held aloft in a photograph that accompanied "Gays Under Fire," a *Newsweek* article on advances and losses by the gay and lesbian community. The role of religion in the contemporary anti-homosexual movement is both real and misunderstood.[1]

The purpose of this chapter is not to refute the sentiment expressed by this placard insofar as it articulates the belief of the man holding it. There is compelling evidence that the god some people worship does hate gays and lesbians, and they remind us of this whenever the subject of gay and lesbian equality is raised. Under our constitutional system, however, one person's protected religious beliefs are not permitted to subvert the constitutional rights of others. It is this very subversion that is the aim of the religious right, as exemplified in its Bible-based attack on gays and lesbians. The First Amendment to the Bill of Rights protects not only religious belief but also speech and thought, which are essential to the flourishing of individual freedom. The disestablishment clause serves a double purpose: It protects religion from intrusion by the state and, by fostering religious freedom for all without ascendancy for any, it protects the state from the warring religious interests that have bloodied history and continue to do so today.

The protection of individual religious liberty was a high priority to the American founders. The principles of human liberty and equality enunciated in the Declaration of Independence and the Constitution were inspired in part by religious belief. It was Jefferson, accused during his life of atheism, who identified the "Creator" as the source of those "inalienable rights" among which were "life, liberty and the pursuit of happiness." The notion that people are created equal implies that there is a Creator for whom no human creature is in some ultimate fashion superior to his or her fellow human creatures. Contemporary fundamentalist politicians seize upon this reference by Jefferson to argue that what the founders intended was a specifically Christian nation whose laws were to be guided by fundamentalist interpretations of the Bible. Nothing could be further from the truth.

Jefferson's religious affiliation and views remain something of a puzzle to historians, but one thing that can be said with certainty is that he was not, in any sense of the phrase, a fundamentalist Christian. A central theological tenet of fundamentalist Christianity is the acceptance of Christ as one's savior which, perforce, assumes the divinity of Christ. You must, Pat Robertson writes, "receive [Christ] as your Lord and Savior." Jefferson did not. As Garry Wills observes in the book *Under God,* "Jefferson's views were sufficiently unorthodox for him to take care that they not become generally known." Quoting Jefferson's own writings on the subject, Wills shows that he had "concluded that Jesus was 'a master workman' at forging and ethical teaching (sic)" and "that his system of morality was the most sublime probably that has ever been taught." This view of Christ stopped short of a belief in Christ's divinity.[2]

Jefferson was a deist. In 1822, three years before his death, he wrote a friend: "The pure and simple unity of the creator of the universe is now all but ascendant in the Eastern states; it is dawning in the West, and advancing toward the South; and I confidently expect that the present generation will see Unitarianism become the general religion of the United States." Jefferson's veneration of Jesus of Nazareth as a great moral teacher who preached monotheism was matched by his opposition to "the corruption of Christianity." To John Adams, he wrote: "The mild and simple principles of the Christian philosophy would produce too much calm, too much regularity of good, to extract from its disciples a support to a numerous priesthood, were they not to sophisticate [Wills reads "contaminate"] it, ramify it, split it into hairs, and twist its text till they cover the divine morality of its author with mysteries that require a priesthood to explain them. The Quakers seem to have discovered this. They have no priests, and therefore no schisms. They judge the texts by the dictates of common sense and common morality."[3]

This digression into Jefferson's religious views is necessary to correct the false views attributed to him by Christian fundamentalists who seek to convince their listeners that the Jeffersonian doctrine of separation of church and state does not preclude the establishment of a "Christian nation." This unhistorical and incredible claim reveals the shaky basis of fundamentalist political theory. It would be more accurate to claim that Jefferson's very point in his insistence on the Statute of Religious Liberty in Virginia, one of the three things for which he wished especially to be remembered, and which he caused to be engraved on his tombstone at Monticello, was to *prevent* the establishment in the United States of a "Christian nation." For Jefferson, religious liberty was like free inquiry, a protected exercise of the individual's human reason. Orthodoxy of any sort was an obstacle to such inquiry, and religious orthodoxy was Jefferson's model of what free government must at all costs avoid. There were more traditional Christians than Jefferson among the founders (although their religious views cannot be equated with contemporary fundamentalism, which is a twentieth-century phenomenon). Their religious beliefs and traditions certainly informed their political views and consequently also their rebellion against English tyranny and their fashioning of our constitutional system of government. But the influence of their religious opinions did not cause them to countenance the promulgation of religious orthodoxies by this new government. They feared, as Jefferson did, religion as an active participant in political life.

If they believed that their rights as free men were God-given, they did not identify a particular religious tradition or exclusive denomination from which that conception of God arose. They cast their beliefs in universal and not specifically Christian terms, and they refrained from establishing the kind of official state religion that then prevailed in Europe (and, for that matter, the rest of the world). They regarded the demand for religious uniformity as detrimental to individual liberty and believed that no religion could help claiming to be the one, true way. Hence, they realized that to elevate one particular sect would denigrate all others and begin a cycle of resentment and oppression that must culminate in a war of religion. The system they founded erected a wall of separation between religion and government to protect individual religious conviction from government persecution and, equally important, to protect the give-and-take politics of a free people from the uncompromising demands of religious orthodoxy. Enshrined in the American founding is the principle that religion is a personal, individual matter of belief and not part of public business.

We live under the regime of disestablishment that they founded. Does this mean that religious beliefs may not be brought into secular controversies? Of course not; how could they be kept out? Most Americans believe in a God, a Creator, a Prime Mover, a Universal Life Force, or, in the phrase used in the recovery movement, a Higher Power, and the majority subscribe to particular religious traditions or denominations. The individual moral compass is a critical element of citizenship in a democracy, and religion can be a significant part of the formation of that compass. People bring their religions into politics when they use their own consciences to guide their citizenship. Any given religious tradition, however, can produce diametrically opposed political positions among individuals claiming inspiration from it.

History illustrates such intradenominational conflict in, for example, the sectional division of American Baptists over the issue of slavery in the nineteenth century, and the split between the black and white Southern Christian churches during the African-American civil rights movement in the twentieth. Contemporary religious life abounds in internal divisions such as those in the American Catholic church over divorce, contraception, and abortion, and among Jews concerning the ordination of women, a controversy that troubles many Christian denominations as well. The Constitution forbids the government from enshrining a particular religious view, from taking sides in the ever-swirling theological and moral controversies to which religions are prone and which have made religion historically partial to theocracy rather than democracy as a political goal when it had access to civil power.

The controversy within denominations is graphically evident in the differing ways in which religious groups deal with their openly gay and lesbian congregants. Despite the Vatican's official position that condemns homosexuality as an "objective moral disorder," for instance, Catholic priests still officiate at masses held by Dignity, a group of gay and lesbian Catholics; some of those priests are themselves gay. Though the American Baptist Church declares that "there is no scriptural endorsement of homosexual life-styles as Christian life-styles," two Baptist churches in North Carolina have taken the unprecedented step of solemnizing the union of two gay male couples.[4] Even though Orthodox Jewish groups provide the Christian right with some of its most dependable support for antigay positions, there are a handful of gay and lesbian Jewish congregations across the country, and some other Jewish congregations and affiliates are receptive to those groups. Notwithstanding their official positions, American religions are struggling with the issue of homosexuality and the movement for gay and lesbian rights, and their practices often vary from their official positions. These conflicts of conscience and interpretation among and within religions make the religious dogma of any sect a questionable and dangerous source of public policy. Disestablishment purposefully protects this diversity of religious views and allows different religions to work out their own responses to homosexuality, as to other issues.

The same question of acceptance that exists in the church regarding homosexuality exists among lesbians and gays with respect to the church. The church asks, "How can we accept our gay and lesbian congregants and still adhere to our teachings on the subject of homosexuality?" while the gay person asks, "How can I return to my faith and still be faithful to my own self-knowledge?" Underlying both questions is the tremendous desire on the part of some gays and lesbians for affinity to the faiths of their birth or choice. For these gay people, the church is a fount of moral teaching and spiritual revelation, just as it is for their heterosexual counterparts, and their exclusion or self-exile is a source of pain to them. Indeed, some gays and lesbians maintain that without their religious faith, they would never have come to an acceptance of their homosexuality. Chris Glaser, who directs the Lazarus Project at the West Hollywood Presbyterian church, writes:

> *In my spiritual development, I moved from lonely place to lonely place in search of God and in search of myself. I first believed my homosexuality was both sin and sickness. God did not deliver me from my homosexuality, but did free me from my guilt about my condition. Then I believed that my homosexuality was my 'thorn in the flesh' or 'cross to bear.' I suffered from feelings that I could not express, let alone fulfill, and believed that this would shape me into a better Christian. God did not deliver me from my feelings, but did free me to accept the gift of my sexuality. When I fell in love with my closest male friend in college, I cried secretly in the closet. God did not deliver me from my love, but did free me from my closet. As I sought to serve the church in the professional ministry, I felt devastated when denied ordination. God did not deliver me from my calling, but freed me for ministry. Throughout my personal history, prayer offered me the perspective to see what God was accomplishing in and through the lonely places of my life."[5]*

Other lesbians and gay men also question the basis of their exclusion from the community of the faithful. John J. McNeill writes, "When we look at tradition, we find that tradition in turn relies both on a questionable use of Scripture and on a relatively unexamined cultural heritage.... As in many other areas of moral philosophy, the advances made in philosophical anthropology, where the human is understood along dynamic lines of self-creative freedom rather than static essence, serve as a basis for critical reexamination of the traditional condemnation of homosexuality derived from the natural law approach of the Scholastics [e.g., Thomas Aquinas]."[6] In citing this critique of the tradition of scriptural condemnation of homosexuality, we are not using it as an argument in favor of gay and lesbian equality. We look no further than the Constitution. We wanted, however, to show that the issue of homosexuality and religion is far more fluid and evolutionary than is usually acknowledged and that this in itself makes a strong argument for rejecting the static dogma and interested positioning of the religious right as a basis for public policy on the issue. Their resort to the public arena is, in part, a move to resolve outside the churches things that the churches remain divided about. The inevitability of such an attempt shows how prudent is the separation of church and state.

Religions will always resort to external authority to resolve internal disputes. The Constitution says that American democratic politics is not an appropriate arena for such disputes and absolutely protects the individual conscience as the proper arena. What bothers the religious right is that (at least in principle) in this country ideas are equal in the intellectual marketplace. Believing, as an article of faith, that the revealed truths to which they subscribe—and which they define—supersede all other truths, they find the many voices of American pluralism anxiety-provoking rather than healthy. The sounds of democracy ring in their ears like Babel. A

religious interest group characteristically credits itself with a
mission and a motive that are above the criticism that other
political interests take for granted. While other groups seek
to persuade, the religious interest group wants to convert.
The individual conscience is too risky a venue for the zealous
orthodox of any sort, and persuasion is too uncertain a
weapon.

Persuasion does not require that the person persuaded
abandon all previously held beliefs and subscribe to an entirely different set, nor does it assume bad faith or perversity
on the part of the unpersuaded. It is not necessary, for instance, to embrace homosexuality for oneself to believe that
discrimination against others because of their homosexuality
violates their individual freedom. It is possible to dislike gays
and lesbians, and even to believe they are condemned to
hell, and still respect their right to live their lives as they
choose, holding whatever beliefs they do about themselves,
because this self-same freedom protects you in your life and
your beliefs. This differs markedly from the religious right's
position. Religious rightists allow no distinction between
their religious convictions and civil law; if their own religious
tradition condemns homosexuality, the law must therefore
apply that condemnation. This insusceptibility to compromise, combined with the belief of religious interest groups
that a different standard applies to their political activity, is,
of course, the abiding reason for the constitutional separation
of church and state. Establishment is as natural to the religious impulse in politics as monopoly is to the commercial
impulse. But while it is the nature of business to settle for
less as a way of getting as much as it can, it is against the
nature of religious interests to compromise what is never
simply a political position, but a revealed truth.

For this reason, even the freedom that promotes and protects religious expression cannot be left to religion. The freedom to seek spiritual truth has swelled the ranks of American

religion, but other expressions of individual freedom have not always been welcomed by the churches. They look askance at the very climate of pluralism and individual choice that enabled their own growth. They view freedom as existing for the sole purpose of establishing their views. The religious right, in particular, which has profited by our constitutional commitment to freedom, finds it impossible, and not even particularly desirable, to respect its use by others. This strain of religious intolerance has constantly intruded into American political life. Anti-Semitism, anti-Catholicism, and race and gender restrictions have all, at one time or another, been justified as part of a divine order—and still are, among some sects. It was not so long ago that Protestant evangelicals were vocally certain that Roman Catholics posed the kind of threat to their traditional values that they now purport to fear from gays and lesbians.

Jewish fellow-travelers of Moral Majority–like fundamentalists would do well to remember that, despite their historic support for the state of Israel, these fundamentalists and their constituencies have frequently been as anti-Semitic as they are now anti-gay. In 1980, when the Reverend Bailey Smith, then president of the Southern Baptist Convention, remarked, "God does not hear the prayer of a Jew," he was simply, if artlessly, articulating the logical conclusion of fundamentalist theology's insistence on redemption through Christ alone. Even sects like the Mormons and the Jehovah's Witnesses that share the social attitudes of the fundamentalists are condemned by them. Pat Robertson, that exemplar of evangelical orthodoxy, writes that the Mormons "are far from the truth" in spiritual matters, while dismissing Jehovah's Witnesses as being "not biblical." The point here is that, while their targets may change, the purposes of the fundamentalists, and other politically inclined denominations, stay the same: the denigration of differing points of view and the silencing of those who hold them.[7]

The goals of gays and lesbians and those of the religious right are not commensurate. One group aims to extend citizenship and its protections to a community excluded from them for no acceptable constitutional reason, while the other wishes to suppress unwelcome neighbors and their way of life by denying them equal protection of the laws. But equal protection is not determined by majority vote, much less by religious certainty, however vociferously expressed. It exists, in part, to prevent majorities from imposing their will in a way that subverts the liberties of everyone.

2. THEO-POLITICAL CORRECTNESS

American religion has been forced to develop remarkable means of serving the spiritual and moral needs of individuals who are not compelled by law under our constitutional system to seek this communion. The result of disestablishment is that religion flourishes—"religion" understood as *religions,* as the variety of creeds and observances that individuals, families, and groups adopt to guide their moral and spiritual lives. Many religions, from Protestant sects to the Roman Catholic Church, have used this freedom to exercise significant religious traditions that had been the object of pre-Revolutionary restrictions and post-Revolutionary bigotry. The power of the Protestant fundamentalists (not to mention their sometime religious allies) derives from their appeal to individual men and women, who are, in our constitutional system, the ultimate judges of spiritual and moral truth. Outside of theocracies, few nations can boast a comparably healthy religious life.

Once solidified, however, these religious groups tend to look askance at the climate of pluralism and freedom responsible for their success. It is always easier to learn to use freedom than to respect its use by others. In the contemporary lexicon of the religious right, "pluralism" is a dirty word, a concept on which it blames the woes of modern society. Gary Bauer, a domestic policy adviser to Ronald Reagan, wrote: "Pluralism is cited as the reason we must show infinite tolerance for all views and viewpoints—except those based on tradition and a Judeo-Christian ethic."[8] But the viewpoint that Bauer, and other religious-right leaders espouse, based on "tradition and a Judeo-Christian ethic" as they define them, excludes any other viewpoints.

In a pluralistic society, people act according to their own views of right and wrong, except where their actions violate agreed-upon criminal codes. This moral diversity is precisely what the religious right objects to; rather than seek to persuade nonbelievers of its version of the truth, it would simply impose that version on them. It was for this reason, rather than hostility to religion, that the founders put up, in Jefferson's phrase, a wall between church and state. They shared the view that a government based on the will of a free people was incompatible with an official role for religion. History had taught them that the possession of religious truth impels the believer to political action on the basis of that truth. And unless the public arena is one in which people agree to disagree on religious belief, violence is certain to follow. The purpose of the separation of church and state was to keep religious passion from overwhelming the public life of the new nation as it had in Europe in previous centuries of religious warfare and persecution.

The First Amendment, insofar as it treats religion, ensures everyone's freedom of conscience by prohibiting the establishment of religious opinion by the state, even if that opinion happens to be a majority opinion. Under our Constitution, respect for the moral views of the religious is not the same thing as believing that those views must prevail in public debate because they are invested with greater authority than other moral views. The hard choice the Constitution makes is to protect individual religious observance and the religious groups, but not to open the public arena to the establishment of religious orthodoxy. Whatever the elements that forge the society's common morality, the government under our Constitution cannot promulgate religious opinion even though it takes the presence and good effect of religion for granted. The theory of separation of church and state is that religion will thrive and teach people right from wrong, while the public arena will benefit from that teaching without attempting the hopeless and divisive task of enacting it.

Intentionally or not, the founders created in American constitutional principle a secular ideology—a civic myth— that could unify people of disparate religions without requiring them to surrender their beliefs. *E pluribus unum,* "Out of many, one," is not a spiritual adage, but it serves the same function in public life, reminding Americans of a commonality that both transcends individualism and celebrates it. The system works through compromise. What it holds sacred is the individual's right to private belief. What it fears is the attempt by one group or another to impose its sacred beliefs on everyone else. Religious belief characteristically requires an individual's submission to a particular creed to the exclusion of all others. The believer cannot compromise those beliefs because adherence to them is the key to salvation, which is the highest goal of human life. The problem is complicated further by the proselytizing impulse of most religions. Christianity, Judaism, and Islam link the fate of the individual to the state of the community in which the individual resides. In Western religious tradition, you are your brother's keeper. At its best, this tradition promotes reform, good works, and concern for others, but at its worst it leads to intolerance, intellectual narrowness, and the persecution of nonbelievers; one need only look at Iranian theocracy and the sectarian violence in Northern Ireland, the former Yugoslavia, and India for proof of this proposition.

The Constitution favors no one form of religious expression over any other, but it does restrict religion to the private sphere. Far from being antireligious, this proscription was intended to preserve freedom of religious expression and protect the civil peace. Religion holds power under this system not because of the sacredness of its tenets but because religious expression is protected. That is, religion has a status similar to that of individual freedom and must abide by the restraints that this system of rights imposes. Just as individual rights to freedom of speech do not include the right to yell "Fire!" in a crowded theater, so freedom of religion does not include the right to banish people who happen not to share your own religious views. Religion enjoys freedom, not a license to interfere with other people's freedom.

The religious right's complaint that Christian values have been left out of public discourse reveals either a basic misunderstanding of our constitutional system or an equally basic disregard for its principles and workings. It is certain that the founders did not envision a republic without moral values that powerfully inform public discourse. But it is also clear that these values were for the individual to hold, and that public discourse had to be stated in terms susceptible to compromise, so that the arguments were about the public interest, not religious truth. Religious-based values are not banned from the public arena, but they are not vested with any greater moral force than competing viewpoints, nor are they exempt from rational examination simply because they originate in someone's notion of the divine. The religious origin of opinion does not, in our system, give the opinion any special status in public debate. In a contest between individual freedom and particular religious views, individual freedom must be preferred because it and its corollary, equal protection of the laws, are what the American constitutional system holds sacred.

In this sense, the empowerment of the individual by a church is fundamentally different from the empowerment of a citizen within the American constitutional system. Even religious views are seen by the Constitution as expressions of individual freedom. The individual mediates the relation of church and state; neither church or state can dictate moral views to the individual except by the individual's consent or participation in the common moral life of the community. Moral values are not ineligible for public discourse, but their enactment into law is a secular matter, not a religious one.

The relation of these observations to the religious right's opposition to gay and lesbian equality is as follows: No one disputes the right of individual members of the religious right to oppose gay citizenship on the basis of their interpretation of certain biblical passages. But the claim—as it happens, a disputed one—that these views about citizenship reflect biblical, hence divine, revelation gives the rightists' argument no special weight. Scriptural views are not exempt from dispute and have no special status within our constitutional framework. The (dubious) claim advanced by the religious right that it represents a majority's views—also has no standing; it violates exactly the tradition of separation of church and state and infringes on the individual's essential rights even in the face of majority opposition.

The religious right's active opposition to gay rights is based on two points. The first is a shared belief that homosexuality is bad and that homosexuals should therefore be denied equal protection of the laws. (But the fact that the holders of this opinion trace their belief to their own religious views does not give their view equal status with the claim of lesbian and gay American citizens to full rights as citizens.) Second, it is evident that the religious right regards the issue of gay equality as a means through which it can impose a radical reinterpretation of the American constitutional system and its history to support the claim that the United States is a "Christian nation," as defined by the right's own views. Both points equally endanger individual freedom in the United States. It is, perhaps, easier for non-gay Americans to see how the second attacks on their own freedom of conscience by manipulating an outmoded cultural prejudice against homosexuals in order to impose a narrow and intolerant religious orthodoxy on everybody. To resist the religious right on the issue of gay equality is not an attack on religion but, among other things, a defense of real religious liberty.

3. FROM FLAPPERS TO QUEERS

The religious right comprises more than Protestant evangelicals, but it is they who have been in the forefront of the movement and particularly insistent in their opposition to gay and lesbian rights. The fundamentalist movement (here we use "evangelicals" and "fundamentalists" interchangeably), insofar as it has intruded itself into politics, is motivated less by theology than by its long-standing distrust of individual freedom and its opposition to modernity. Though it derives some of its political principles from its selective interpretation of biblical texts, it should not be regarded simply as a religious movement but as a social and political movement as well. Other Protestant denominations draw their inspiration from the same biblical texts and yet come up with opposite conclusions about issues ranging from abortion to gay and lesbian rights to sex education. The Episcopal Church, for instance, has ordained gay and lesbian priests; several denominations bless and acknowledge gay and lesbian unions, and many Protestant churches welcome homosexual congregants and minister to the particular needs of lesbians and gay men. Notwithstanding the fundamentalist claim that it does not interpret biblical text but simply applies it, fundamentalism is, in fact, an interpretation of the Bible, and only one of many.

With their roots in the itinerant and populist strains of

Protestant sectarianism, the evangelicals who lead the religious right have always purported to believe that the end of the world is at hand. From this perspective, social reform and the liberating possibilities of individualism have always seemed wrongheaded, even dangerous and heretical. Radical mistrust of the modern world and of its preoccupations with material progress, social tinkering, and, above all, individual conscience as the key site of moral reasoning, has been the rallying cry of fundamentalism since its emergence in its modern form from 1880 to 1920.

Fundamentalism was a Bible-based, Bible-belt answer to the flappers, radio, dancing, urbanization and other changes that facilitated the personal enjoyment of modern American life. Frances Fitzgerald writes,

> *Fundamentalism and Pentecostalism went against much of what has long been assumed to be the American grain: faith in science, faith in the power of human reason, and faith that man can improve the conditions of life on earth. At the core of fundamentalist theology was the doctrine of Biblical ignorance, the doctrine that held every word of the Bible to be the word of God and literally, historically, true. Thus, Creation occurred in exactly six days some ten thousand years ago. . . . True fundamentalism saw the world as one of sin and suffering, one that even Christians could do very little to improve given the frailty of human nature. In their theology the one important task for a Christian was to bring as many people to Christ as possible.* [9]

The roots of modern fundamentalism lie in the response to modernity of Dwight Moody, William Jennings Bryan, Billy Sunday, and their fellow-travelers on the what-has-the-world-come-to circuit. To make their point, they required a text and they needed an illustration. The text remained the

Bible—and the more fundamentalist the preacher, the textier the preaching. But the appeal of an antimodern message to those who felt left out required a token of the times. Thus, the flappers and the cities could symbolize for the fundamentalists of the twenties the disarray and dislocations of their own times.

As this description suggest⌐, while early fundamentalists used the modern world for purposes of comparison to the kingdom of God that was promised to the saved, they remained largely apolitical. Some scholars suggest that they became political after the Scopes trial. The anti-communism of the 1950s repoliticized some of them. When the African-American civil rights movement emerged from the black church in the south, white fundamentalist leaders deplored the use of religious morality and imagery to advance a political cause, and at the same time some exploited anti-communism as a technique for undermining the civil rights movement. The split between Billy Graham and Martin Luther King, Jr., over the role of Christianity in the perpetuation of racial prejudice and segregation represents another point at which white fundamentalists turned away from solutions to social problems in favor of a Bible-based effort to will them away or, at best, of a private and individual salvation focused on moral rather than social reforms.

In a famous 1965 sermon called "Ministers and Marchers," Jerry Falwell, who concedes he was a segregationist at this point in his career, preached that nowhere in the Bible "are we commissioned to reform the external. We are not told to wage wars against bootleggers, liquor stores, gamblers, murderers, prostitutes, racketeers, prejudiced persons or any other existing evil as such. . . . Believing the Bible as I do, I would find it impossible to stop preaching the pure saving gospel of Jesus Christ, and begin doing anything else—including fighting Communism or participating in civil-rights reforms."[10] Falwell, for one, has given various explanations for his radical shift from nonparticipation in politics to his deep enmeshment in them, but the answer probably lies in what happened in this country during the 1960s and 1970s.

Prior to these decades, the fundamentalists could rail against the state of modern America, but in important respects, most Americans continued to subscribe to moral beliefs that were not much different from those of the fundamentalists. These beliefs were reflected in laws that banned abortion, made divorce difficult, criminalized adultery and sodomy, and enforced racial segregation. The social effect of these laws was to keep most women in traditional roles, enforce religion-based sexual morality, keep African-Americans subservient to the white majority, and make gays and lesbians fearful and inconspicuous. But in the sixties and seventies millions of Americans, particularly young Americans, questioned the basic assumptions on which society operated and, as they moved into and influenced the political system, began to change the rules on the basis of a liberationist vision of human potential. Fundamentalists saw the ground shift from beneath them as not only their theological beliefs but their social beliefs and manner of living were increasingly marginalized.

When leaders of the religious right talk about "traditional" values what they mean is the world as it existed before 1960—that mythical period of American history, represented by the Eisenhower presidency, of social calm and unanimity. As James Dobson, a pediatrician and founder of the religious right group Focus on the Family remembers it,

> *I attended high school during the "Happy Days"*
> *of the 1950s, and I never saw or even heard of*
> *anyone taking drugs. . . . Some of the other stu-*
> *dents liked to get drunk, but alcohol was not a big*
> *deal in my social environment. Others played with*

*sex, but girls who did were "loose" and not re-
spected. Virginity was still in style for males and
females. . . . Homosexuals were very weird and
unusual people. I heard there were a few around
but I didn't know them personally. Most of my
friends respected their parents, went to church on
Sunday, studied hard enough to get by, and lived
a fairly clean life.*[11]

It was a period of white, male, conservative, Christian, heterosexual hegemony during which the claims of those who
were different could be ignored with impunity and they
themselves dismissed as "weird" or "loose" or "uppity."

It is easy to see why this mythic fundamentalist utopia
appealed to millions of Americans in the late 1970s and early
1980s, when the country was exhausted by the turmoil of the
preceding two decades, divided in its assessment of the value
of the changes wrought by that turmoil, and fearful of their
consequences. Then, too, fundamentalist leaders like Jerry
Falwell, James Dobson, Francis Schaeffer, Pat Robertson,
Jimmy Swaggart, and Jim and Tammy Faye Bakker were
able to command vast audiences through the "electronic
church" and through direct-mail techniques pioneered by
political right-wingers. In the 1980s the religious right attempted a cultural counterrevolution, assisted first by Ronald
Reagan and then by his successor, George Bush, both of
whom owed their elections in part to the religious right's
organizational prowess. But the counterrevolution did not
occur, not yet, at any rate—and the radical social agenda of
the religious right was sacrificed to politics; indeed, by the
1980s the religious right was transformed into a staple Republican Party special-interest group. Their prominence at
the 1992 Republican Convention had much the same effect
on middle America as the dominance in 1972 of perceived
countercultural Democratic party interest groups: It turned

voters off. The religious right is a less formidable presence on the national scene since the election of Bill Clinton. But it has redoubled its already formidable and formidably funded efforts at the local and state levels, working to capture control of state and local Republican Party apparatus, controlling school boards and city councils and pushing initiatives like Colorado's anti-gay amendment. It remains to be seen what effect these determined efforts to build a power base in the state Republican parties will have nationally.

Because the religious right remains a potent force, particularly in its opposition to gay and lesbian equality, it is worth emphasizing what that force represents. The religious right is a counterrevolutionary movement whose purpose is to return society, and the individuals who make up society, to the social understanding and the roles that existed in the 1950s. It is not difficult to determine what society would look like if the fundamentalists won political primacy. Falwell, Robertson, Bauer, and others have, in their writings, suggested what the ultimate political goals of their movement are. Reproductive freedom would be overturned by denying women access to birth control, including abortion. Attempts would be made to confine women to the home whether they wanted to be there or not. As Pat Robertson has written to justify his position against the ordination of women: "God has established a pattern. He is the head of man and man is to be the head of woman, and together they are to be the head of children. This does not mean that a woman cannot be a business executive or a politician or a lawyer, but in the government of the family and the church, men are to be the leaders." This perfunctory nod to women in the professions acknowledges the many powerful women in the religious right, like Beverly LaHaye, whose sensibilities Robertson might otherwise offend. But, as Charles Colson writes, "God has ordained three institutions for the ordering of society: the family for the propagation of life, the state for the preservation of life, and the church for the proclamation of the gospel. These are not just voluntary associations that people can join or not as they see fit." Edward Hindson, a family guidance counselor at Falwell's church put the matter more bluntly in a book called *The Total Family:* "The Bible clearly states that the wife is to submit to her husband's leadership and help him fulfill God's will for *his* life" (our emphasis). It is clear from statements like these that in a fundamentalist regime, the role of women in public life would be much diminished.[12]

We may also anticipate the enactment or reenactment of laws governing sexual morality in light of fundamentalist interpretations of scripture; anything the Bible calls sin in the arena of sexual morality would be reflected in civil and criminal law. Adultery would be recriminalized and laws would be passed making cohabitation a criminal offense because, as Robertson writes, cohabitation—which he calls fornication—"is a sin against the body." Additionally, divorce laws would be rewritten to make divorces much harder to obtain, except on grounds like adultery, because fundamentalists take the view that the only legitimate grounds of divorce are spelled out in the Bible. By reintroducing the concept of blame, which modern divorce statutes omit, such laws would also have consequences for child custody and spousal support. Of course, sodomy laws against gays and lesbians would be enforced or reenacted, and all existing antidiscrimination laws would be repealed. A constitutional amendment like Colorado's could be passed that would specifically prohibit legal protections for gays and lesbians. Indeed, some of Falwell's associates in the now-defunct Moral Majority, would have gone further and required the death penalty for homosexuality.[13]

New definitions of pornography would overturn Supreme Court formulations that allow each community to determine its own standards of explicitness. These new definitions would be narrower in scope and lead, for instance, to the removal of works by great American authors from public libraries, something that now occurs on a smaller scale across the country. There would, of course, be censorship boards for film, theater, music, and the visual arts. Any government spending on the arts would be determined by clerical prejudice, not truth, interest, or artistic merit. The religious right would reinstate prayer in public schools, and, given the complexion of its leadership, that prayer would likely be Christian. The government might require that religion be taught and it would certainly censor school texts, or rewrite them, so as to avoid any challenges to its political authority. These texts would go far beyond granting parity to evolutionary science and creationism. The crusade to replace secular with religious education in the public schools would resolve any inconsistencies between fundamentalist Christian religion and secular education in favor of religious opinion.

The religious right would erase the distinction between church and state in public service and government since, as Falwell writes in explaining his political activism, "it was my duty as a Christian to apply the truths of the Scripture to every act of government." Doubtless, because some of its supporters come from the African-American church and community, the fundamentalist government would leave intact basic civil rights laws, but would nevertheless narrow their scope. In the 1980s the religious right was allied with those political conservatives who eviscerated laws that extended equal economic opportunity to minority ethnic and racial communities. There is a powerful political dimension to the religious right's politics that has more to do with Caesar and Mammon than with God. Finally, it would seem inevitable that Christianity, as interpreted by Protestant fundamentalists, would be recognized, if not established, as the nation's official religion.[14]

The rough coalitions of right-wing and evangelical entrepreneurs and fundamentalist Christians who make up the religious right describe themselves as concerned Americans who have been activated by radical assaults on traditional morality from homosexual activists, the latest in a long line of subversive elements who pose a threat to American moral order. The image they project is of ordinary folks speaking from family homes and small churches. In fact the religious right is a group of mail-order wizards and lobbyists tied to religious "media personalities" who spend millions to raise millions with the twin object of advancing their own social and political agendas and enriching themselves and their organizations. Their frantic campaign against the extension of equal protection of the laws to gay and lesbian Americans is being conducted with a veritable avalanche of publications, direct-mail solicitations, and scare publications of all sorts. It is not possible to digest the whole campaign, but some excerpts from the spectrum of religious anti-homosexual mailings suggest the character of the arguments being made.

Salt, "the Washington Newsletter of the Christian Life Commission of the Southern Baptist Convention," restates in a 1993 issue its view of homosexual rights:

> *The CLC opposes homosexuality, because it is clear in the Bible, God condemns it as a sinful lifestyle harmful to the individual and society. Therefore, the CLC opposes the granting of civil rights normally reserved for immutable characteristics, such as race, to a group based on its members' sexual behavior. . . . The CLC proclaims the gospel because the Scriptures declare the Lord Jesus can change homosexuals. To accept homosexuality as an appropriate, alternative lifestyle would betray the life-changing sacrifice of Christ and leave homosexuals without hope for a new and eternal life.*

The editor of the self-described "independent religious publication" *The Reformer* answers the question "Why do you oppose homosexuality" as follows: "Because God condemns it, and heaven's testimony denounces it. Additionally, homosexuality is physiologically unnatural, unsafe and harmful. Death is usually the result." The editor does not himself sit in judgment on gays; "God sits in judgment on homosexuals. We are at liberty to inform them how God feels about the sexual scourge, as the apostle Paul did." The privately printed tract *The Truth About the Homosexual* (sent to one of us in response to a newspaper commentary on gay rights) answers the question "What does God think of homosexuality and lesbianism?" this way: "He hates it!" and continues: "I believe the aids [*sic*] epidemic, we see mostly in the homosexual community, is the judgment of God on these people for their vile sin. God even refers to them in some passages of the old testament as dogs, because they perform the sex act like dogs. God hates homosexuality!"[15]

In *Family Voice*, published by Dr. Beverly LaHaye's Concerned Women for America, an article exposing the magazine *Junior Scholastic* for advancing the "gay agenda" singles out the inclusion of "sexual orientation" as a characteristic of people against whom hate crimes are frequent. "For instance," staff writer Marian Wallace pointed out, " 'hate crimes' was defined as: 'crimes motivated by the victim's race, religion, ethnic background or *sexual orientation*.' And while hate crimes can never be condoned, the intent was clear—that homosexuals should be considered a minority, like a racial, ethnic or religious minority." The article's tangled reasoning proceeds to define the attempt to educate children to resist bigotry against, among others, homosexuals as somehow alienating the children from their parents and home values. The point, of course, is to remove gays from the list of people crimes against whom constitute hate crimes. Acting out one's hatred of homosexuals is acceptable behavior in the world of the religious right.[16]

The religious right is working furiously to deny homosexuals equal protection of the laws, and one strategy is to decriminalize hate crimes against gays and lesbians. It is a fine point of religious reasoning that distinguishes between the failure to consider crimes against gays hate crimes and the encouragement of attacks on gays because God hates their sinful ways. The evidence is unmistakable, however, that perpetrators of hate crimes against gays routinely cite religious reasons for their hatred of gays. Those of us who have published opinion pieces in favor of gay equality can testify that most of the hate mail we get cites religious justifications for the hate. One recent piece, on AIDS education in the work force, elicited an anonymous response, which was scrawled across the article: "Jesus Christ—son of God—tells us 'I shall not allow to scientists to find a cure for the Plague of AIDS because of the horrible actions which cause it!' " This sentiment may not represent the views of all those on the religious right who have targeted gays and lesbians, but it is the kind of view licensed by the intrusion of their religious beliefs into the public debate.[17]

It is worth pondering how even the most well-disposed person could respond to an argument from scripture, to the assertion that God wills this or that belief. Imagine arguing with someone like the anonymous annotator of this recent opinion piece. Theologians have had little success in reconciling differing interpretations of the holy word, and history reveals little precedent for the peaceful resolution of such debates; schism is more common than compromise in the history of revelation on earth. One can fight about such views or agree to disagree, but they are almost by definition outside the conversation of civil society. And although the target of the moment for the organized coalition of the religious right is lesbians and gays, they have bigger fish to fry. So get used to their goals, to their views of the right society, to their picture of family values.

The opposition to gay rights is the advance guard of the religious right's wholesale invasion of the political life of this country. Any attempt to solve pressing social issues by recreating an imaginary past will only serve to erode or eliminate much of the personal freedom that most Americans take for granted. There is no question that issues like pornography, drug abuse, and poverty present challenges that seem, at times, insurmountable. But they cannot be dealt with simply by turning the clock back forty years to a time that never really was. Although gays are the present targets of the counterrevolution, the rest of America is not far behind. Remember, it is the religious right that has declared a "cultural war" on the rest of us. James Dobson and Gary Bauer also talk about "the second great civil war," as does Charles Colson, Watergate felon and reborn Christian activist. Pat Buchanan's martial imagery at the Republican Convention in August 1992 was deliberate; it expresses the way that the leaders of the religious right think about the rest of us. They are more careful than they once were to disguise their broad agenda. The Republican Convention was a tip-off the likes of which they cannot afford again. It was like the moment at the end of the movie *A Face in the Crowd* when Patricia Neal leaves the mike running so that listeners can hear how contemptuous of his devoted fans the populist country boy played by Andy Griffith really is. In August 1992, Americans got to hear how things will sound if the religious right and its allies get the kind of power they want.

The religious right rejects cultural pluralism and it rejects individualism. It sees its opponents not as fellow Americans presenting alternative views of what American society might look like; it sees them as conscripts in the army of Satan. And lest you think this is mere rhetorical indulgence, here's Pat Robertson on "demons": "Just as the angels have archangels and higher powers, the demons have what are called 'principalities and powers.' It is possible that a demon prince is in charge of New York, Detroit, St. Louis or any other city. Particular sins are prevalent in certain cities. One might have rampant homosexuality, while another may be troubled by excessive lust."[18] Plainly, such an apocalyptic approach to social issues is principled in its insusceptibility to reason and compromise, the basic tools of democracies; in this respect, the ideology of the religious right is profoundly antidemocratic. Such paranoiac politics represent a grave danger to the Constitution and the society it informs, far graver than the imagined danger represented by constitutional equality for gays and lesbians.

4. THE WORD OF GOD, SOMETIMES

In *Spiritual Warfare,* her study of the religious right, Sara Diamond noted that a *Christianity Today* survey of evangelical pastors and their flocks reported that 35 percent of those pastors admitted either being sexually inappropriate, or having sexual intercourse, with someone other than their spouses, while 68 percent of their congregants made similar admissions.[19] On one level, these figures simply demonstrate the degree of moral hypocrisy of segments of the religious right, but on a different level, they may explain some of the ferocity with which fundamentalists conceive of sexual impropriety in others, and especially gays and lesbians. What Mario Cuomo asked in his address on Catholics and abortion has some relevance here: "Are we asking government to make criminal what we believe to be sinful because we ourselves can't stop committing the sin?" Much of the religious right's attack on gays and lesbians seems to be fueled by this preoccupation with what they conceive to be their own and others' moral weakness in the sphere of sexuality.

This explains why the religious right frames its opposition

to gay and lesbian civil rights in voyeuristic, obsessional spec-
ulation about the sexual practices and designs of lesbians and
gay men. For example, the Oregon Citizens Alliance, the
anti-homosexual front group that sponsored the unsuccessful
anti-gay constitutional amendment in that state, asserted in
its propaganda that "homosexual men, on average, ingest the
fecal material of 23 different men per year." By such out-
rageous statements, the religious right attempts to frame the
debate over gay rights as a referendum on sexual practices,
real or—as is most often the case—fabricated in the overripe
imagination of some evangelist. They do this to associate the
ordinary rights of homosexual Americans, which most other
Americans have few passionate feelings about one way or
another, with images that will incite Americans against gay
rights and against gay people. They also appear to be satisfying some needs of their own; for all their talk about promiscuity and "the homosexual lifestyle," it is the religious right
that italicizes sexual practices. Of course the real debate has
never been about whether people should have homosexual
sex, or sex of any kind. The issue is whether American citizens are to be allowed to make their own decisions about
their lives without fear of retribution from the state.[20]

The emergence of an openly gay and lesbian population
is simply the latest stage of the evolution of individual liberty,
and a reaffirmation of American tradition. The decision to
accept one's homosexuality is untainted by power trips or
the desire to convert the world. Gay men and women don't
come out because it's fashionable, popular, easy, safe, man-
datory, or conventional; they do it to be true to themselves.
It is crucial to recall that the fundamentalist forces of "tradition" attack gay life as they and their ancestors have attacked American secular life for decades. Having gone from
dancing to electricity to flappers, they are still here and they
have settled on gays and lesbians. They are committed to a
view of life in which their own salvation is undermined, un-

less the state they live in mirrors their moral preferences. They believe that freedom outside of a biblically dictated Christian moral order is the root of all evil; they think that political freedom cannot be entrusted to morally free citizens. Their unease about freedom strikes a responsive chord in other groups understandably uneasy about the consequences of freedom. It is possible to be concerned about freedom, to be in this sense conservative, without buying the bogus claim that sexual orientation describes the fault line of American social health. For instance, Barry Goldwater argued that permitting gays to serve openly in the military would strengthen the defense posture of the nation—and Andrew Sullivan has argued that gay marriage would strengthen America's moral fiber. In this sense, conservatives have as much to fear from the distortions of the anti-homosexual religious right as do the rest of us.

History moves in cycles of freedom and distrust of freedom. In our own time, the collapse of totalitarian communism and the revival of democratic hopes worldwide coexists with a powerful fundamentalist impulse that challenges the very premises of liberal democracy. In the United States, religious fundamentalism has set its sights on secular power; its purpose, like that of religious fundamentalism everywhere, is to control the behavior of all citizens. The religious right aims to convert traditional principles of toleration and personal liberty to Bible-based precepts of "revealed" behavior and comprehensive social order—"revealed," that is, to a few preachers and evangelists, and to their strategists, fund-raisers, and media advisers.

There is no doubt that the evangelical attack on gay and lesbian rights is part of a broader strategy to impose specifically religious values on American politics and American bodies. We have already imagined the fundamentalist dystopia. Gays and lesbians make an ideal target for an evangelical coup because of the persistent fear and hatred of homosexuality in our culture. It is much easier to say "gay" or "lesbian" in denunciation than in pride or even as a matter of course. Much of the work of the gay and lesbian movement has been to accustom people to saying the words. How many parents find that they can't quite get their mouths around the words "My son is g-g-gay" or "My daughter is l-l-lesbian"? The religious right's fight against reproductive freedom may be floundering in part because people are accustomed to saying "abortion" without having to mumble, let alone whisper.

It is the goal of the gay and lesbian movement to make "gay" and "lesbian" words one expects to hear, registers, and considers without reluctance. At this point, the religious right still controls those words. Its members say "homosexual" in tones that unnerve and frighten people, playing on their fears and their habit of regarding homosexuality as something strange and secret. But, as any gay person can testify, the words are only scary until you get used to saying them. The aim of the religious right is to terrify people with the specter of predatory homosexuality in order to assert control over public morality. The fear of homosexuality is being used to make ordinary people conspire in their own moral disenfranchisement. The sectarian disapproval of homosexuality, however genuine and supported by personal belief, is different from a statutory prohibition against it. The First Amendment does protect the right of people to their own negative opinion of homosexuality. What it does not protect is the enactment of that opinion into laws that regulate other people's lives and free expression.

Many Americans are intimidated by the religious right's facile citation of the Bible in support of their denunciation of gays and lesbians. Reverent about the Bible, yet unfamiliar with the text, much less with contemporary exegesis, they are easily silenced when an evangelical quotes the famous lines from Leviticus: "Thou shalt not lie down with mankind as with womankind: it is an abomination," or invokes Sodom and Gomorrah or some phrases from St. Paul. Modern biblical scholarship and historical studies of Christianity take issue with both fundamentalist Biblical exegesis and the notion that Christianity has always been hostile to homosexuality.

According to a recent essay by Peter Gomes, professor of Christian morals at Harvard University, and himself a Baptist minister, nine passages are commonly cited as indicating biblical responses to homosexuality. Four, Deuteronomy 23:17, I Kings 14:24, I Kings 22:46, and II Kings 23:7 forbid male and female prostitution, not same sex love. Leviticus 18:22 and 20:13 (the passage quoted above) do explicitly forbid homosexuality; but Leviticus also prohibits adultery, the eating of raw meat, tattoos, intercourse during woman's menstrual period, the planting of two different kinds of seed in the same field, and other everyday behavior. Anthropologists, historians, and theologians have long since established that the Levitican codes have to do with purity and tribal identity rather than sin. As historian John Boswell explains, the Hebrew word commonly translated as "abomination" does not usually signify something intrinsically evil, like rape or theft (discussed elsewhere in Leviticus), but something which is ritually unclean for Jews, like eating pork or engaging in intercourse during menstruation, both of which Leviticus proscribes. "Abomination" is used throughout the Old Testament to designate sins that involve ethnic contamination or idolatry, and very frequently occurs as part of the stock phrase "toevah ha-goyim," "the uncleanness of the Gentiles" (see, for example, II Kings 16:3). Boswell shows that homosexual acts are discussed in the Old Testament only in the elaborate sections concerning the many things that distinguish the community of Jewish believers, and not, as is now regularly asserted, as a prohibition based on the intrinsic evil of the act.[21]

The point here is to clear up the misconception that the Bible singles out homosexuality as an intrinsically evil act—as it does incest, adultery, and murder, for instance. Boswell's work, and that of other scholars, shows that human rather than divine revelation is the source of the view that homosexuality is sinful and evil and as such can be treated as a human choice, to do or not to do. The work of these scholars also suggests how inappropriate religious arguments are in the constitutionally mandated forum of civil discourse. How can the courts, for instance, take Levitican prohibitions of various forms of ritual uncleanness, meant to distinguish the ancient Hebrews from their neighbors, as grounds for denying equal protection of the laws, when, as it happens, they do not do so with the specific moral evil of adultery? Religion does not lend itself to such discussion; that is its great spiritual and moral strength and its essential problem as a principle of civil society.

Jesus of Nazareth had nothing to say about homosexuality, if the four Gospels of the New Testament are to be believed, for there is no mention of homosexuality in them. Paul does condemn homosexuality (Romans 1:26–27, I Corinthians 6: 9–10, and I Timothy 1:10). Peter Gomes and many other contemporary biblical scholars, construe these passages contextually to emphasize that condemnation of homosexuality was part of the strategy of the early Jewish Christian movement to counter the secular sensuality that characterized Greco-Roman culture. Paul denounced sensuality and lust in everyone. "To say that homosexuality is bad because homosexuals are tempted to do bad things is to say that heterosexuality is bad because heterosexuals are likewise tempted. For St. Paul anyone who puts his or her interest ahead of God's is condemned, a verdict that falls equally on everyone."[22]

One is free to accept or reject Paul's understanding of the dangers of sensuality to spiritual redemption. It is a common perception among the religious that the claims of the body are at odds with the demands of the spirit. It is a different matter, however, to twist this into a specific denunciation of homosexual as opposed to heterosexual sensuality, as if heterosexuality were somehow less sensual than homosexuality. Such denunciations are a common strategy of homophobic bigotry, and are no more valid in biblical criticism than in social description. It is equally troubling to think of this partial reading of Paul being asserted as a sensible basis for denial of equal protection of the laws to American citizens who are homosexual.

Perhaps the favorite biblical citation of those who oppose equal protection of the laws for homosexuals is the story of Sodom and Gomorrah (Genesis 18–19). "Is it any surprise that God decided to bring judgment upon the homosexual communities of Sodom and Gomorrah? Then why should we think it a surprise that today he is bringing judgment upon the homosexual community in the form of AIDS?" is a characteristic use of the text. As it happens, the story of Sodom and Gomorrah is not a story about homosexuals, despite the linguistic coincidence that the word for various sexual acts, including some homosexual acts, is derived from Sodom.[23]

John Boswell describes how the sexual understanding of the Sodom and Gomorrah story was primarily the creation of the later phases of the formation of Judeo-Christian orthodoxy and its concentration on sexual purity. In the Old Testament, it remains a story of breached hospitality. This is not the place to detail the interpretive controversies that swirl around this text. It is, however, appropriate to the issue at hand to emphasize that the notion that Sodom was destroyed because of homosexuality is, at the very least, very controversial among biblical scholars, and hardly a sound basis for denying citizenship in the United States. Jesus never spoke about homosexuality, but, as Boswell points out, he did refer to Sodom and "apparently believed that Sodom was destroyed for the sin of inhospitality: 'Whosoever shall not receive you, nor hear your words, when ye depart out of that house or city, shake off the dust of your feet. Verily I say unto you, It shall be more tolerable for the land of Sodom and Gomorrah in the day of judgment, than for that city' (Matthew 10:14–15)." This is consistent with the fact that the numerous references to Sodom in the Old Testament do not in any instance specify the Sodomite sin as homosexuality.[24]

Whatever one decides to believe about Sodom and Gomorrah, however, the controversy surrounding the story underscores both the reasons for and the wisdom of the American founders' choice to separate church and state and to protect religion as a private matter rather than as a public authority. The Bible is there to guide individuals in their moral and religious lives and it will continue to lead them, as it always has, to different choices, affiliations, and beliefs. The Constitution is there to protect them in their free exercise of that religion. The Constitution is also there to protect them and everyone else from anybody's attempt to impose a particular interpretation of any sacred text on others. Again, the principle of separation of church and state would obtain even if the Bible were the tract against homosexuals that the religious right claims it is. That it is certainly not and that there persists irresolvable controversy surrounding the issue gives us renewed understanding of the prudence of the constitutional position that personal liberty is incompatible with theocracy.

John Boswell summarizes the problem of attributing the social alienation and disenfranchisement of gays to the sacred truths of religion:

> *Religious belief may cloak or incorporate intolerance, especially among adherents of revealed religions which specifically reject rationality as an*

ultimate criterion of judgment or tolerance as a major goal in human relations. But careful analysis can almost always differentiate between conscientious application of religious ethics and the use of religious precepts as justification for personal animosity or prejudice. If religious strictures are used to justify oppression by people who regularly disregard precepts of equal gravity from the same moral code, or [if] prohibitions which restrain a disliked minority are upheld in their most literal sense as absolutely inviolable while comparable precepts affecting the majority are relaxed or reinterpreted, one must suspect something other than religious belief as the motivating cause of oppression.

The religious right fails both of Boswell's tests, and the flawed integrity of its position reveals how dangerous a guide to common morality its campaign is.[25]

There is another reason to suspect anti-homosexual activists' resort to biblical texts. Such citation in the service of politically repressive measures has been seen before in American history. Numbered among the forerunners of the present-day fundamentalists were the southern preachers who justified the practice of human enslavement by quoting yet another passage of Leviticus: "Both thy bondmen, and thy bondmaids, which thou shalt have, shall be of the heathen that are around about you, of them shall ye buy bondmen and bondmaids. . . . And ye shall take them as an inheritance for your children after you, to inherit them for a possession, they shall be your bondmen forever . . . " (Leviticus 25:44, 46). As historian Shelton Smith writes, "The southern churchman . . . contended relentlessly that the master-slave relation was explicitly sanctioned in both testaments of the Bible, and consequently to denounce that relation as sinful was to impugn God's word." Although Leviticus explicitly sanctions it, even the most fundamental of the fundamentalists would doubtless refrain from advocating a return to slavery, while continuing to denounce gays and lesbians on the basis of the same book. Here is a good instance of Boswell's test to differentiate between sincere application of religious ethics and their use to justify personal prejudice; the same text is cited for one proposition but the second, equally explicit one is ignored. This, of course, is the dilemma of fundamentalism. If every word of the Bible is true, then fundamentalists must perforce advocate human slavery and prohibit the wearing of garments made of more than one kind of yarn. They get around the dilemma by pretending it does not exist, but the rest of us must think carefully about their hermeneutical inconsistency as we consider their biblical claims in respect to morality and homosexuality.[26]

It bears repeating that fundamentalism is but one of many strains of Christianity, not all of which share the fundamentalist view of homosexuality. A wide spectrum of opinion runs from the American Baptist Convention's position that "there is no scriptural endorsement of homosexual life-styles as Christian life-style" to the statement of the British Friends that "surely it is the nature and quality of a relationship that matters; one must not judge it by its outward appearance but its inner worth. Homosexual affection can be as selfless as heterosexual affection, and therefore we cannot see that it is in some way morally wrong." The condemnation of homosexuality by some churchmen does not mean either that their congregants refrain from homosexuality or that it is the unanimous view of all religions that they should. These variations in views support the wisdom of the constitutional principle of separation of church and state. Since no unanimity exists on the subject, no one sect's interpretation should form the basis of civil government.[27]

The Reverend Mel White was an important player in the religious right's crusade. He ghost-wrote Jerry Falwell's autobiography, *Strength for the Journey,* and his book about abortion; he wrote Pat Robertson's *America's Dates with Destiny* and Billy Graham's *Approaching Hoofbeats;* he wrote speeches for Oliver North. White was a closeted gay man during those years. He has since come out and is now a minister with the Metropolitan Community Church. The irony of a gay man ghost-writing the tracts of the homophobic religious right is interesting to savor, but not all that surprising, after all, in a culture that has always depended on its outsider groups to help define the inside. White bears important direct witness about the motives and purposes of his onetime associates: "These guys are not interested in biblical truth. They are only interested in proving, through their interpretations of the text, their own prejudice." The anti-homosexual part of their crusade is just the first step. They hope to take advantage of the indifferent, ignorant, suspicious, or bigoted attitudes of heterosexuals toward homosexuals to begin their "moral cleansing" of the American population. They trust in heterosexual indifference to the fate of the homosexual in the same way that ethnic and racial demagogues expect broad bonds of ethnic or racial solidarity to blind people to the tyranny being erected in their name. A large-scale division of the population into straight and gay will serve the long-range interests of the religious right. Theirs, not gay activists', is the radical constitutional position. The religious right has discovered homosexuality as a marketing tool, and we may expect them to feature it, partly to intimidate homosexuals but principally to scare the freedom out of everyone. To protect their own individual freedom, not to mention traditional American democratic pluralism, Americans will have to recognize their gay family, friends, and neighbors as fellow citizens.[28]

FIVE

The Ghost in the Machine

1. THE INCREDIBLE SHRINKING HOMOSEXUAL

N₀ ONE KNOWS HOW many gays and lesbians there really are in this country. The 10 percent figure commonly advanced by lesbians and gays themselves reflects a common understanding of the results of Alfred Kinsey's post–World War II survey of American sexual practices and refers to that survey's estimate that "10 percent of the males are more or less exclusively homosexual . . . for at least three years between the ages of 16 and 55." A study released in 1993 claimed to revise the Kinsey findings with an estimate that gay males accounted for only one percent of the population. In a response to this and other studies that found significantly lower estimates of homosexuality among men and women, Paul H. Gebhard, former executive director of the Kinsey Institute for Sex Research and professor emeritus of anthropology at the University of Indiana and himself a noted sex researcher, observed that despite certain methodological flaws and some disproportionate representation of certain populations, the key figures in the Kinsey study remain "close to the truth." At this point, then, 37 percent of Americans of both sexes have had at least one homosexual experience. Ten percent of white educated men have been more or less exclusively homosexual for significant periods of their adult life. Gebhard restates his conclusions from a 1972 National Institute of Mental Health study that 4 percent of college-educated white males and 2 percent of college-educated white females are "predominantly homosexual." Obviously much research remains to be done, and the too familiar class, gender, and race biases of scientific research must be corrected. But recent studies that significantly understate the Kinsey estimates are themselves seriously flawed. Random sampling does not account for established patterns of homosexual migration to big cities. In addition, the extensive interviews that characterize the Kinsey surveys are more likely to reveal the kind of information about which subjects are likely to be reticent, such as homosexual identification in a homophobic society, than polls conducted by researchers at best only slightly acquainted with the techniques and methods of sexual survey. Gebhard's conclusions are worth restating because they remain the closest to authoritative we have on this subject: "In summary, Kinsey's two famous figures, despite their methodological flaws, are not bad estimates of reality and can be used for practical purposes in determining social policy . . . "[1]

The real story behind the furor that followed the one percent study is not how many gays and lesbians there are, but how the percentage has been made part of the debate on gay equality. Gays understandably stress the larger percentages, in part because they know how many lesbians and gay men remain in the closet, prudently hiding themselves from public notice. Heterosexuals, for their part, seem in general to need to believe that homosexuality does not exist except in a tiny, aberrant segment of the population with which they have nothing in common. This view, which sees gays not as part of the American community deserving of all the rights and privileges of citizenship but as a "special interest" whose demands can be dismissed because of their numbers, represents a significant impediment to their struggle. Not merely their entitlement to basic rights, but their very existence is questioned.

To some extent, this invisibility is due to the nature of homosexuality, which is generally undetectable unless someone chooses to come out. In *The Invisible Man* Ralph Ellison illuminated the process by which society marginalizes and exploits its others, leaving them out of the cultural representation of reality, making them feel invisible. The persistent animus against homosexuality not only causes the majority culture to ignore gays and lesbians, except as stereotypes, but terrifies lesbians and gays into remaining in the closet. It would be easier for the cause of gay rights if all gay people identified themselves so that heterosexuals could see how many of their own are gay. But because self-identification would also make gays and lesbians a much easier target for gay-bashing, most are afraid to make the fact of their existence known. While remaining in the closet is prudent survival strategy, it also makes closeted gay men and women hapless collaborators in their own oppression. More relevant than why gays and lesbians remain in the closet is the question of what function the closet serves for the heterosexual majority.

The short answer is that if gays and lesbians were acknowledged, and their lives legitimated by the culture, it would interfere with heterosexist socialization, or what the poet Adrienne Rich calls "compulsory heterosexuality."[2] Everyone, whether or not heterosexual, is conscripted into the ranks of heterosexuality. Lesbians and gay men are saturated with images, products, incentives, and rewards that encourage heterosexuality; they are bombarded with gender stereotype and heterosexual conditioning. A staple of the commercial in this most commercial of cultures is the selling of products by means of heterosexuality (and perhaps vice versa). The not so subliminal theme of a large percentage of American advertising is gender identification and heterosexual conditioning: This is how boys and girls grow into men and women, this is how men and women go about it, this is what a woman must to do attract and keep a man and what a man must do to woo and win a woman, this is how little boys and little girls should practice being men and women interested in women and men, ad infinitum.

Since these outward images correspond to their inner desires, most heterosexuals see nothing remarkable in such representations. To them they are merely cultural reflections of "natural" sexuality. But homosexuals notice what heterosexuals do not—not only that these images fail to represent homosexual desire, but that homosexual desire is ruthlessly expunged from them. Why, one must ask, if heterosexuality is "natural," is all this effort being expended to promote it? Is it because what is being promoted is not natural sexuality but a form of social organization that excludes those to whom its promotions are not addressed?

The anti-gay right, oddly enough, understands this as most of the heterosexual world does not. The theory of "homosexual recruitment" advanced by them to oppose gay and lesbian rights rests on the premise that sexual desire is amorphous and can be channeled into homosexuality as easily as into heterosexuality. Thus, because anti-gay rightists believe that "the homosexual lifestyle is based on the recruitment and exploitation of vulnerable young men," homosexuality must be suppressed to save all those sad young men. In fact, however, heterosexuals are not recruited by homosexuals; rather, *homosexuals* are recruited by *heterosexuals* almost from the moment they are born. The homosexual recruitment fantasy is simply one more instance of how heterosexuals project their own behavior onto the victims of that behavior as a justification for persisting in it.[3]

Scientific investigation into sexual orientation suggests genetic predisposition for it. The question being posed, predictably enough, is "Why are people gay?" rather than "What is the nature of sexual orientation?" This kind of science, it should be noted, has analogies to race science of the late nineteenth and early twentieth centuries: it attempts to investigate difference as a deviation from some norm, when all there is is difference. Science knows little about what it actually means to call a trait genetically innate. Human knowledge about how genes work, how the brain works, and how the combination of elements we name "desire" works is scant, pitifully short of something to draw conclusions from.[4] Nevertheless, the early results of this work do suggest genetic links to sexual orientation. This has brought great relief to many homosexuals, who appear to take this new information as confirmation of what they know about themselves: that being gay is the way they are, not a choice they have made. The idea that homosexuality is genetic appears to make many people more comfortable with their own homosexuality and that of others, probably because the cultural conditioning to regard homosexuality as a sinful, chosen behavior is so strong that it takes "science" to refute it. We begrudge no one the comfort they find in these indications. The movement for gay equality will be strengthened by the empowering character of lesbian and gay people's reading of these data and by the recognition on the part of heterosexuals that "gay," like "straight," is a state of conditioned being, not a lifestyle choice.

One of the oddest things about the claim that one chooses to be gay is that the lesbian or gay person cannot track having made the choice. Who chooses sexual orientation? Who chooses the object of desire? The choice is, of course, not to desire but to act on it. It has never really been central to the argument against gay people's existence that being gay is a choice. The Catholic Church has always granted, for instance, that same-sex love was a natural condition in people; the church still calls it sinful to express this natural orientation. Even the establishment of some biological determination of sexual orientation with scientific evidence does not go to the heart of the constitutional issue.

Similarly, accounts of how gays and lesbians "got to be that way" is not really germane to the argument for equal protection of the laws—or at least it should not be—although it may well help to lessen the pervasive atmosphere of hatred or indifference regarding homosexuals and their human and civil rights. The issue is an issue of choice, protected choice. The choice to venture one's sexuality in intimate association is a choice that is protected by our regime, and the legal equality between homosexual and heterosexual choice in this matter is what is at stake. Homophobia considers only gayness a choice, because it is a different option from the majority one.

The discouragement and discrimination society offers as impediments are not really there to turn gays straight. The superstructure of discrimination is there to recruit people away from their own natures and to prevent lesbians and gays from living their sexual orientations. The stake heterosexuals have in this process is properly the subject of another book. It is akin to the stake whites have in degrading nonwhites, men in degrading women: what the demeaning of any class of difference does to promote the majority group's feeling of superiority. It may even be necessary for the minority to be stigmatized for there to be a majority. Certainly it takes a lot of recruiting to create heterosexuals. Calling gays sinful gives straights a shortcut to feeling superior. Any serious attempt to establish superiority on the basis of heterosexual identity is absurd, which is why the claim must be advanced through prejudice, superstition, repetition, and intimidation.

Whether it turns out that sexual orientation is in one's hardware or software, a genetic predisposition, a social formation, or some combination of innate with learned and voluntary behavior, the relevant choice is the one to live as a gay person in this society with all the rights that citizenship confers. This choice is one that many fear. It is, however, the choice lesbians and gay men make and, having made, will not unmake. It is a choice that is protected by the constitutional guarantee of equal protection of the laws. It does challenge the heterosexual myth that has beguiled this culture for so long, revealing it for the nonsense it is. It may turn out to be true that the category of "homosexual" itself merely serves to restrict polymorphous human sexuality into the artificial divisions of gay and straight. For now, we are stuck with the category and its attendant civil impediments, and we can say that the homosexual category does not constitute a justifiable exception to the equal protection of the laws, or individual liberty.

Even if it is not accompanied by the homosexual-recruitment fantasy, the notion that human desire is amorphous is one of the powerful anxieties underlying compulsory heterosexuality. This anxiety can be dispelled, however, by simply looking into one's own mechanism of desire. While many people do feel an erotic attraction for someone of their own gender at some point in their lives, rarely is the attraction strong enough to be acted on, or, if acted on, powerful enough to persist in over a lifetime. Most people do not organize their lives around fleeting sexual desire, but on the bedrock of their basic orientation. A mass gay and lesbian movement has existed in this country for twenty-five years, but there is no evidence that the incidence of people identifying themselves as homosexual is any greater than it was when Kinsey took his survey in the 1940s. Homosexuality is plainly not attractive to people who are not homosexual. Accordingly, there is no justification for attempting to channel all sexual desire toward heterosexuality. It doesn't makes straights straighter; it only makes the lives of gays and lesbians more difficult.

The promotion of heterosexuality serves another purpose

than that of soothing heterosexual anxiety: It encourages family formation and domestic life. As we have already made clear, we think the promotion of family is a legitimate goal of society. But "family" need not mean the traditional heterosexual family to the exclusion of all others. If the function of family is to channel sexual expression in a way that promotes social stability and provide a place in which children can be reared and acculturated, then same-sex families are as capable of fulfilling those functions as mixed-sex families. (We are not suggesting, of course, that these are the only functions family serves, only what people generally mean by "traditional family values.") Instead of taking an inclusive view of family, however, the culture takes a narrow view that conflates family with heterosexuality, narrowing even that definition to exclude single-parent families. The destructive effects of this persistent illusion are everywhere around us.

Because gays and lesbians are the ghost in the machinery of heterosexual conditioning, their existence must either be denied or made menacing. The expunging of homosexuality from official texts accomplishes the former; stereotypes produce the latter. Stereotyped representations of lesbians and gay men also arise from the ideology of heterosexuality, which posits not only a single "natural" sexuality, but "natural" gender roles as well. Stereotypic beliefs about gays and lesbians are as much about gender as they are about sexual orientation. They promote the same conventions of masculinity and femininity that women have had to struggle against in their quest for equal citizenship. The "bulldyke" of popular culture—the warden of a B-movie set in a women's prison, say—stands as a warning to women of the consequence of stepping outside the roles that society allots them. Similarly, the "queen"—effeminate, fussy, ridiculous—functions as a kind of cultural scarecrow warning men away from critical explorations of the conventions of masculinity.

Men and women are so intimidated by the fear of being

thought homosexual if they step outside their gender roles that they remain imprisoned by them. In a society where heterosexuality was not the *sine qua non* of maleness and femaleness, this fear would evaporate and people would be freer to be themselves. The distinctions that would persist between people would reflect individual differences rather than stereotypes of gender and sexual orientation. The "masculine" woman would not represent the demonic face of feminism; she would simply be part of the spectrum of femaleness. The "queen" would not be an emblem of masculinity traduced; such a man would be nothing more than one of the kinds of men that maleness comprises.

These spectrums already exist; the stereotypes serve the majority culture's need to describe such unconventional maleness and femaleness even while denigrating and caricaturing them. Liberace's notorious appeal to middle-American, middle-aged women with his flamboyantly effeminate and elaborate self-presentation bears thinking about. The odd elision of his homosexuality was the only thing not explicit about this remarkable performer. He must have represented something his women fans wanted in their lives. So long as the effeminacy and homosexuality of his public self was not mentioned, Liberace filled a cultural niche of some importance. There is no shortage of other such representations, from Franklin Pangborn and Jack Benny to Truman Capote. Our purpose here is not to identify these public performers as gay or not, but to think about why effeminate males are such a staple of popular culture.

One reason, of course, is that they do exist, just as homosexuals of every stripe exist, despite the culture's code of silence. The other reason is that such men are welcomed by many—especially, but not only, by women. The society's official gender roles impose too-narrow confinements on real people. Thus the feminized man represents something the culture needs but cannot easily represent, because it needs to acknowledge that all men possess, to one extent or another, such "feminine" qualities as sensitivity and emotionalism. On the other hand, this tacit admission comes with a warning not to go too far. So the gentle, sensitive man becomes encumbered with aspects of hysteria, flamboyance, and ridicule.

The existence of gays and lesbians who do not fit these stereotypes presents the culture with a dilemma it solves by denying that they exist. To acknowledge their existence would challenge prevailing assumptions about family and even more deeply held views about gender roles. The central mandate of the gay and lesbian rights movement is to issue such a challenge. Sooner or later the culture will have to respond, either with greater inclusiveness or increasingly repressive measures against its homosexual minority.

2. IN THE COURT OF PUBLIC OPINION:
GAYS AND THE MEDIA

The immediate events that inspired us to write this book were the 1991 demonstrations in Los Angeles following Governor Wilson's veto of a gay-inclusive anti-discrimination bill and the virtual news blackout of those demonstrations by the city's paper of record, the *Los Angeles Times.* For two weeks, thousands of gays, lesbians, and heterosexual men and women flooded the streets of the city, bringing parts of it to a standstill. It was the longest and one of the largest gay rights demonstrations in history, in the city many historians see as the birthplace of the modern gay movement.[5] Yet the *Times* quickly relegated the demonstrations to its "Metro" section, signaling to the national media that the story was of local interest only. Its editorial coverage, which alternated between berating the demonstrators and wondering what political effect the demonstrations would have on the governor's political fortunes, at best missed the point and at worst

showed an anti-gay bias disturbing to gay and lesbian readers
who had welcomed the paper's often sympathetic cultural
coverage of their community. The *Times*'s coverage of the
demonstrations suggested to those readers that while gay
men and women occasionally made interesting feature copy,
as a political force they were no more than a fringe group.
Although its editorial coverage of the gay and lesbian community has improved, largely because of the demands of its
gay and lesbian reporters for greater visibility on the op-ed
pages—the *Times*'s overall coverage remains abysmal. It is a
sorry comment on mass media coverage of lesbian and gay
news that the *Los Angeles Times* is by no means the worst
offender in perpetuating the invisibility of gays and lesbians
and particularly of their political concerns. Indeed, the *Times*
probably ranks better than most.

The gay and lesbian community continues to be covered
in a sensationalistic way that usually misunderstands the fundamental issues of individual freedom and equality at the
heart of the gay rights struggle. One illustration of this was
the media's coverage of the issue of outing, a practice
whereby some gay activists revealed the homosexuality of
public figures associated with anti-gay policies. *The Advocate*
revealed the homosexuality of Pete Williams, the Pentagon's
top civilian spokesman in the Bush Administration, who was
allowed to keep his sensitive position despite the Administration's policy of ferreting out and discharging gay and lesbian servicepeople. Although outing was controversial in the
gay and lesbian community, it was at least understood to
serve the political purpose of drawing attention to official
hypocrisy on the subject of gay and lesbian rights. The mainstream media, ignoring this underlying issue, condemned
outing in often vitriolic terms, typically comparing it to Mc-
Carthyism, a misnomer of staggering dimensions. The media
managed to miss even the point of their own comparison—
that being identified as a homosexual is as potentially de-

structive of someone's career as being called a Communist was in the fifties. Rather than address this cultural terror of homosexuality, the media preferred to address sanctimonious lectures to gay and lesbian activists on their tactics.

USA Today, a paper generally fair on gay and lesbian rights, opined, "Outing violates the right to privacy at the heart of gays' claim that they should be able to live as they wish." Such a statement reveals the fundamental ignorance with which the media address the issues raised by the gay rights struggle. The right *to* privacy to which these editorialists refer and the constitutionally protected right *of* privacy are two different creatures. The latter is the right of people to openly identify themselves as gay and lesbian and make decisions affecting their personal lives without fear of retaliation by the government. The right *to* privacy as put forward by *USA Today* is the "right" of people to lie about, or hide, their sexual orientation so as to escape the penalties that usually follow disclosure.[6]

In this society, the concept of privacy as it relates to gay men and women has been turned on its head. The Supreme Court has ruled that the state may invade the bedrooms of gay people and arrest them for private, consensual sexual acts, but the public disclosure of a person's homosexuality may well be an actionable invasion of privacy. Indeed, a New York court not so long ago held that "a false charge of homosexuality is defamatory."[7] Homosexuality is an issue in this society because of the legal penalties and disabilities attached to it, which gays and lesbians must fight to overturn if they are ever to enjoy true privacy, which is another way of saying real freedom. What *USA Today* was offering gays and lesbians is not the right to privacy but permission to "pass," much as some light-skinned African-Americans could pass as white or some Jews as Gentiles.

On the other hand, we do give *USA Today* credit for taking the issue seriously and attempting to formulate a response to it, something that only a few other major news outlets bother to do, most prominently *The New York Times* and *Newsweek*. In one survey, 77 percent of 227 senior newspaper editors conceded that their gay and lesbian coverage (as distinct from coverage of AIDS) was fair or poor, which is probably a generous estimate. For the most part, the mainstream media pursue a policy of alternately defaming or ignoring significant numbers of their consumers.[8]

When lesbians and gay men seek to address their fellow citizens through the media they find themselves in a double bind. In order to gain a public hearing, they are commonly expected to "debate" people who regard homosexuality as a sin and homosexuals as unnatural perverts, not American citizens. The result is that serious discussion of homosexual Americans, and the discourse of civil rights that might emerge from that discussion, are too often over before they have begun. Most discussions become unedifying encounters with radical antigay activists whose agenda is, simply, the obliteration of gay people. Imagine a situation in which, in order to articulate their positions on matters of equity or public policy, African-Americans were routinely required to answer the claims of white supremacists, or Jews the anti-Semitism of neo-Nazis. This is what gay men and women are regularly expected to do to win access to the media. It is impossible to have a serious conversation with people who refuse to admit your humanity or even your right to exist, much less your equality before the law. We are not challenging the First Amendment rights of homophobes to air their prejudices. What is at stake is the justice of requiring homosexuals to answer these prejudices as if truths about our lives were equivalent to prejudice against us.

The media, reflecting society at large, maintain rough guidelines for the airing of irrational prejudice. White supremacist racism, for example, appears in news coverage and serious talk shows as something to be analyzed and denounced as a phenomenon everybody deplores. The views of the racists are offered up as examples of positions society finds unacceptable in a democratic state. Skinheads are questioned the way criminals are: "Why do you hold these bizarre views?" "What makes you do these crazy things?" It is a sorry fact that prejudice against gays, and the violence it engenders with increasing frequency, are not yet treated by the media with the same clarity that racism, anti-Semitism, sexism, or discrimination against the disabled are. Issues of equity and polity are not regularly distinguished from the grossest expressions of prejudice.

Gays and lesbians who remark upon and protest this situation are given the same unreflective response. "Balance," they are told, requires that those who oppose gay civil rights be given the chance to respond to the claims of gays and lesbians. But opponents are often responding to an entirely different set of questions. Balance requires reasonable and opposing views within the broad context of public debate being given commensurate exposure. The problem with "balance" as it is applied to gays is that their claims to individual liberty and equal protection of the laws are equated with the views of those who are simply prejudiced against them. The consequence of this distorted view of balance is that gays are continually required to battle hate simply to address issues of justice and equity. All prejudice needs is a slogan to invigorate the emotions that work its will. To argue against prejudice takes time and effort, because the debate must be translated from the sphere of received opinion into that of rational discussion. Prejudice doesn't advance rational discussion, but subverts it. This principle is recognized when the rights of every significant minority group except gays and lesbians are at issue. Then, ignorance and prejudice are routinely vented in the name of a balance that is totally unbalanced.

A good example of this dynamic is what happens when the

most respectable of current homophobic slogans, "gay lifestyle," is injected into public debate, as it was last year by
President Clinton. "Gay lifestyle" is a phrase promulgated
by the antigay right to alarm heterosexual Americans by associating gay civil rights claims with extreme sexual practices.
Building on years of prejudice, "gay lifestyle" summons a
host of negative and fearsome stereotypes to the public
mind. But gays cannot respond to a catch-phrase like this
with another catch-phrase. It takes time to deconstruct the
term's surface plausibility and untangle the supporting system of prejudice.

There is no such thing as a single "gay lifestyle," any more
than there is a single "straight lifestyle." If people believe
there is something common or even typical in the way that
gays and lesbians live, they should be required to define it,
not merely bandy about a slogan. If, for example, by "gay
lifestyle" one means "sexual promiscuity," then one should
have to say that in one's opinion sexual promiscuity (which
one should also be required to define) disqualifies a person
from citizenship. Of course, if this were admitted, the
speaker would also be forced to concede that sexual promiscuity is not the special province of gays and lesbians. This
same analysis holds true for all the elements suggested by
the phrase, including stereotypes. Should effeminate men be
denied equal protection of the law, for instance, or mannish
women? Should childless couples be denied the right to
marry? Are children born to gay parents, and the families
thereby formed, less entitled to the protections and benefits
extended to families in general?

Of course, people get into the habit of using phrases like
"gay lifestyle" without even knowing what they mean. (Did
the President really know what he was saying? Probably
not; he was just using the going phrase to reassure a potential constituency that his support for lifting the ban on
gays and lesbians in the military didn't mean he failed to

respect their prejudices. Would Bill Clinton respond similarly, we wonder, to the claims of an anti-Semite who denied the existence of the Holocaust? Would he reassure such a person of his respect for that person's ignorance and bigotry?) Sure enough, this manufactured anti-homosexual slogan is already making its way into legislation and the political lexicon because it has become a media staple and has passed unchallenged into the language of the moment. Reporters ought to challenge people who use such shorthand to say what they mean, to worry them as would surely be the case if the code were masking racism or anti-Semitism. But reporters as a rule do not ask questions that challenge routine prejudice against homosexuals.

It is left to lesbians and gay men to do the challenging, and the only location available is still an arena of combat rather than a forum for serious discussion. Responding to antigay buzzwords can exhaust available space, not to mention the attention span of readers and auditors. For other groups, the media enforce boundaries they do not enforce for gays. Reasonable people cannot be expected to have to forestall prejudice in order to make arguments. The conversation must be with those who raise issues about *how* the society will accommodate the claims of its gay and lesbian members, not with those who deny the seriousness of those claims because of their own ignorance and hatred of homosexuality. So long as the public debate about gay rights equates the claims of gay Americans with the prejudices of those who hate homosexuals, public discourse about the issues arising from those claims will be stalled. The media must move beyond prejudice and shock value to consider how gays and lesbians will be integrated into the American mix. Most gays and lesbians are eager for this discussion. They have it among themselves all the time, and gay and lesbian views differ as widely as do gay and lesbian lives. Many lesbians and gay men are eager to make the case for our civil rights and to go their contrary American way after that.

Reform and civil rights movements always change the nature of the debate in a democratic society, introducing new participants in civic discourse, raising new concerns and, understandably, new fears. But the price all of us have to pay for freedom is the uncomfortable accommodation of the apparently different within the circle of people we must regard as equals. The respect for others as equal before the law is a fundamental demand of democracy. Lesbians and gays deserve this respect. We grant it to our most vociferous opponents. We do not demand that they be silenced, only that we be fairly heard. True balance does not require that we be forced to encounter at every turn of public debate assertions that question our right to be part of it. It is time we stopped having to answer the claims of those who see our very existence as an affront. In order for that to happen, the media will have to extend to us the same privilege it does to others whose civil rights are under challenge: the opportunity to engage in a serious conversation with our fellow citizens about our share in our common democratic heritage.

3. THE LESSONS OF A HIDDEN HISTORY

The majority culture's attempt to deny the existence of gays and lesbians is doomed to failure because gays and lesbians do exist, have always existed, will continue to exist, and are increasingly vocal about their existence. For many years, the single most potent weapon in the armory of invisibility was the shame with which gay men and women were taught to regard their sexual nature. What kindles the fury of the antigay right at the gay and lesbian claim to equality and freedom is the implicit rejection of that shame. The energy released by that triumph over shame are what makes the movement so powerful. The gay and lesbian movement signals the existence of a people who have decided that they know more about themselves than what has been shoved down their throats by an ignorant and fearful society. In *The Jewish Pariah,* philosopher Hannah Arendt wrote of the oppressed: "Honor will never be won by the cult of success or fame, by the cultivation of one's own self, nor even by personal dignity. From the 'disgrace' of being a Jew there is but one escape—to fight for the honor of the Jewish people as a whole." Like the Jews of Arendt's description, gays and lesbians have learned that the only escape from the "disgrace" of being queer is to fight for the honor of the entire queer nation.[9]

If most Americans could acknowledge that gays and lesbians are being punished for a sexuality that is as natural as their own, and that this persecution extends to people they know, to members of their own families, to their neighbors and co-workers, they would be hard pressed to tolerate persecution, much less to participate in it. It would be difficult for Americans to believe their fellow citizens should be persecuted for something as normal and familiar as homosexuality really is. Opponents of gay rights, therefore, have to keep America thinking that being gay is something out of the ordinary, new, unfamiliar, something the majority of Americans couldn't get used to. The strategy of the anti-gay right, therefore, has been to keep gays a dirty secret, and in this effort they have been abetted, unwittingly or not, by all those people and institutions who insist homosexuality is a "private" matter despite a political system that singles it out as grounds to deny American citizens their political rights.

This hypocrisy was nowhere better illustrated than in a comment by former President George Bush, who, when asked what he would say to a gay grandchild, replied: "I'd love that child. I would put my arm around him. I would hope he wouldn't go out and try to convince people that this was a normal lifestyle, that this was an appropriate lifestyle, that this was the way to be. But I would say, 'I hope you don't become an advocate for a life style that in my view is not normal, and propose marriages, same-sex marriages as a normal way of life.'" In other words, "I'd still love you if you were gay, honey, as long as you kept your mouth shut about it. Don't think the way you are is normal, because I know what normal is for you, better than you do. Don't go around trying to make the world an easier or safer place for yourself and people like you. Don't try to normalize your life by establishing a relationship, let alone by seeking the sanction of God and state in trying to live a moral life. Do this for Grandpa, who loves you."[10]

Too many gay men and women have parents and grand-parents, aunts, uncles, brothers, sisters, who, like George Bush, substitute willful ignorance and convention for real love and loyalty. For the George Bushes of the world, family values depend on suppressing homosexuality; as a result, the family has been where most gays and lesbians have had to learn how isolated they are. Is there any other group of oppressed people who could not even count on the protection of their own families—who, indeed, experience their families as the cutting edge of persecution?

To those who actively prefer gays and lesbians to remain invisible, history offers a potent lesson of just how much of the civilization they enjoy is the creation of gay men and lesbian women. We recognize, of course, that historical figures may not have identified themselves by the present-day terms "gay" and "lesbian," but those terms are accurate on the evidence these people have left of their lives. The historical record, it is also true, has often been purged in the matter of gay and lesbian history; much has been lost, and much kept secret. The role of sex itself is problematic in recognizing gay and lesbian historical figures. Since homosexuality is still conventionally regarded as being purely sexual in nature, where there is not definitive evidence of sexual activity the implications of behavior can be ignored or denied. J. Edgar Hoover made sure there was no evidence of sexual activity between himself and his lifetime partner, Clyde Tolson. Yet all indications are that their relationship was a homosexual one.

Since, moreover, gays, like everyone else, run the gamut of sexual expression and partnership, it can be difficult to find even outward evidence of homosexuality. Francis Cardinal Spellman, for example, unlike his political ally Hoover, pursued sexual encounters rather than enduring relationships. Their common enemy, Eleanor Roosevelt, cultivated her lesbian relationships within the context of a long-standing marriage. Despite the ways in which they disguised or adapted their homosexuality, the fact remains that our history is populated with gay men and women. Our point is to remind our reader, who may claim not to know any gays or lesbians, how many he or she numbers among historical and cultural acquaintances.

It is hard to imagine American literature without Walt Whitman, Herman Melville, Henry James, Hart Crane, Willa Cather, Amy Lowell, Gertrude Stein, Langston Hughes, Paul and Jane Bowles, James Baldwin, Gore Vidal, Elizabeth Bishop, Allen Ginsberg, Frank O'Hara, John Ashberry, Janet Flanner, Lorraine Hansberry, May Sarton, Truman Capote, Adrienne Rich, and James Merrill, to name only some of the most notable. George Santayana, Carl van Vechten, Alain Locke, F. O. Matthiessen, and Newton Arvin were crucial to the definition of American civilization. American theater is inconceivable without Clyde Fitch, Thorton Wilder, Tennessee Williams, William Inge, and Cheryl Crawford; American music without Stephen Foster, Lorenz Hart, Cole Porter, Aaron Copland, Samuel Barber, Marc Blitzstein, Leonard Bernstein, Virgil Thompson, John Cage, Stephen Sondheim; American art without Thomas Eakins, Charles Demuth, Marsden Hartley, and Ellsworth Kelly. Try to think of American film without Ramon Novarro, George Cukor, Tyrone Power, James Whale, Cary Grant, Montgomery Clift, Greta Garbo, Marlene Dietrich, and Rock Hudson to name only some.

One cannot be an American without having learned about life, values, truth, and beauty from gay men and women. Yet these are the same people whose sexual nature debarred and debars them from equal citizenship. One might argue that the denial of their basic rights did not keep these people from their accomplishments. But, as we have shown, denial of rights is simply the most obvious manifestation of a culture in which gays and lesbians are devalued and shunned. One need only read the tortured biographies of some of these great artists and thinkers to learn the full effect of that de-valuation and shame. These names stand as a reproach to the conventional opinion that either acquiesces in or resists gay rights on the ground of putative immorality, sinfulness, or sickness.

Next time you hear a Pat Buchanan condemn gay men and women as immoral, think of Eleanor Roosevelt. Do you prefer Pat Robertson's vision of American moral community to Walt Whitman's? Is Bayard Rustin or Jerry Falwell the better model of citizenship? If you make the effort to sub-stitute for the ominous figure of "the homosexual" the faces of gay friends, colleagues, or family members or, if you think you don't know any gay people, among your revered artists and historical figures, then you will be able to understand that at stake here are the lives of valuable, irreplaceable hu-man beings, not some imaginary, shadowy figure lurking at the edge of a schoolyard.

You may also begin to understand, on a personal level, why the question of gay rights cannot simply be dismissed as the private concern of gays and lesbians. As one lesbian executive at American Express put it, "Straight people bring their per-sonal lives to work all the time. They just don't think they do.

Co-workers show pictures of the family trip or brag about how little Suzy got into MIT. If your work is suffering because you're going through a rough divorce, the boss says he understands. But no one knew about it when [a lesbian] manager helped her girlfriend cope with her father's death."[11]

Americans must recognize that the issue of gay rights is a political struggle, not a personal problem, and that it cannot be resolved by telling gay people to keep their sexual practices private. Gay men and lesbians have no privacy. Society intrudes into their lives with all the coercive force of church and state. The majority must also realize that it can no longer pretend that the basic issues involved in the struggle for gay rights are irrelevant to heterosexuals' lives. Individual liberty—the right, as Justice Brandeis said, "to be let alone"— is the foundation not merely of our constitutional system, but of our daily lives.[12] The stereotypes and libels that have been used to keep gay people hidden and disenfranchised do not stand up to rational consideration. We do not expect that if constitutional protections are extended to gay and lesbian Americans, the derogatory stereotypes and beliefs about them will immediately disappear. But if they are ever to disappear, the state must, at the very least, stop perpetuating them by using them to deny gays and lesbians their basic rights. And the media must stop regarding them as equivalent to the truths about the lives lesbians and gay men live and the contributions they have always made to our country. At the very least, gays deserve unimpeded access to the free marketplace of ideas on terms of genuine equality. This is something America can and must provide.

SIX

What Do They Want, Anyway?

1. THE REAL *GAY AGENDA*

T HIS HAS BEEN, OF NE-
cessity, a book about what gay men and lesbians do *not* want.
They do not want to continue through life abused, bashed,
and discriminated against in their own country. They do not
want to labor under the vicious stereotypes that incite violence and justify denial of their civil rights. They do not want
to have to struggle so hard to live their lives. Life is trouble
enough without the distracting burden of defending yourself
from fear and prejudice at every turn.

So what do gays and lesbians want? What do we want?
We want more than the absence of abuse. We want our
rights as citizens; we want the chance to live our lives happily
and morally; we want the chance to make our ways individually and as members of a loosely associated community
without being taxed or pressed into service to support institutions and laws that oppress us. We also want things that
go beyond the cessation of pain. Marriage is crucially important to many gays and lesbians, as is support for their
parenting of children. We want the material benefits society
gives to preserve families; the right to serve openly in the

military, in public life, in entertainment; the right to be open about being gay; the right to genuine privacy, not the secrecy that passes for privacy for far too many of us.

Some of these matters can be legislated or decided by the judiciary, and some cannot, but this is no reason not to effect the changes that are possible. Martin Luther King, Jr., was right when he said you can't legislate the hearts of men, but so was Thurgood Marshall when he added that you can legislate their conduct. We have already witnessed the beginning of the public struggle to end discrimination against lesbians and gay men in the military. The protection of civilians who are lesbian and gay is, if anything, more urgent; it will require amending federal civil rights laws to include sexual orientation as a protected class. Sodomy laws must either be repealed or be overturned by the courts. Initiatives, constitutional amendments, or statutes that, like Colorado's, legalize discrimination against gays and lesbians must be ruled unconstitutional violations of the right to equal protection.

Gays and lesbians must be given the statutory right to marry, to obtain custody of their children if they are fit parents, to adopt, to leave their property to one another at death, to do all the other things that people in heterosexual unions are permitted to do. The accomplishments of homosexual Americans and respect for their lives and their privacy must be taught as part of the social studies curriculum in every public school in America. The epidemic of AIDS must be fought with every resource this country has committed to every other epidemic that has assailed it. These are the things that need to be done to protect gay Americans and integrate them into the society. We are under no illusion that these things will be done in the next ten years or even the next fifty, but they must be done.

The debate about any changes in the power arrangements of the society is always framed in terms of what women, African-Americans, gays, or whatever social minority group want. The fantasies of the Lou Sheldons and William Dannemeyers of the world are consumed with that question. George Bush, Sam Nunn, Bill Clinton, and just about everybody else who isn't gay assumes that what gays and lesbians want is the legitimization and approval of their "lifestyles." This is not entirely correct. Gay Americans have individually and collectively created customs and institutions and families that help give us the solidity and clarity that in our own eyes legitimate our lives. We do not expect American society to give us some seal of approval. It is not within the scope of government to do that. We have our own approval. What we do want is equal protection of the laws and *all* that implies, and we want our fellow citizens to acknowledge that our constitutionally protected choices about what is, after all, our own business should not disqualify us from equal membership in the multitude of American communities.

There will always be lesbians and gay men who prefer a gay-oriented way of living, who live in urban gay communities and pursue the attractions and diversions those communities offer. Other gays and lesbians live lives undistinguished by sexual orientation except in their private lives. Most, of course, will mix the two. We ask and deserve that our fellow citizens recognize our existence and accept us into the common life. This is neither begging for acceptance nor looking for approval. It is the corollary of the Bill of Rights that creates a nation of equals, equally free. The constitutional protections we are entitled to must go along with the effort to educate nongay Americans out of their hostile conditioning. Again, this is not to win approval, but to change perceptions enough to prevent majority prejudices from being acted out against us.

It is incumbent on minority groups to acquaint their fellow citizens with the facts of their lives and to remind their fellow citizens of the elements common to everybody's life. In the end, acceptance does matter—acceptance not of the way other people live their lives, but of their right to live them. This kind of acceptance of our membership in the American family is not, as bigots fear, conversion of heterosexuals to homosexuality, but democratic acceptance, which means that our differences do not disqualify us from the exercise of our rights as citizens. What we seek agreement on, acceptance of, is the proposition that all of us have the right to our own lives without someone battering down the door, calling us names, beating us up, denying us work or shelter or medical care, or refusing to honor our intimate unions.

The zealous opponents of gay rights understand that what we want is to be equal as citizens and to establish the principle of equality between gay and straight lives. What they refuse to understand is what we are really like, because they refuse to understand—or perhaps accept—what people are really like. Pluralism and individualism terrify them, because both present opportunities to which they are afraid to expose themselves or their families, so they believe the answer is to wipe out these things. The fact that this is impossible only redoubles their efforts. They want to keep us the creatures of their own fears and prejudices, the scarecrows of their own furious campaigns against individual liberty and individual freedom of choice about the most important and private matters.

Just as it was once assumed that African-American men lusted after white women and suffragists wanted to be men, the anti-gay lobby seems to think that gays and lesbians want to seduce adult and child alike, recruit new queers, and destroy the family. They think the heterosexual two-parent family cannot coexist with alternative families (Adam and Eve, who were not married and had a troubled family life, are preferable to Adam and Steve). And what do the opponents of our rights think we want *then?* To conquer the world? Redecorate their houses?

The opposition's version of what we want tells you more about what they fear and desire than it does about us. Likely as not, what they fear is their own sexual impulses, but their focus is on seduction and corruption by others. This is interesting psychologically but not of much account otherwise. Gay people are not recruited. Heterosexuals recruit and attempt to convert homosexuals, not the reverse. If the opponents of gay rights are truly concerned about predatory sexual behavior, they ought to educate their heterosexual sons, who are the most likely to grow up to be sex offenders, to respect the physical integrity of women and children.

What gays and lesbians want is for our rights as citizens to be recognized as readily as our responsibilities as taxpayers; we want an end to the systematic discrimination against us on the basis of prejudice whether grounded in religious or other opinion. Our opponents believe we are not fully human and deserve to remain disenfranchised and subject to intimidation and violence. They do not believe the Constitution protects anything that goes against their own selective views of what their religions tell them.

Stated generally, what gays and lesbians want is not very different from what most Americans want: to live as little disturbed by government as possible but secure in the knowledge that social institutions will serve them equally and that laws affecting them will be enforced fairly. We are not asking for "special rights" or special treatment. We are not a special interest. On the contrary, we are the victims of special-interest pleading by our opponents attempting to foist their minority religious views on the rest of us. We are demanding our basic rights, rights that Americans are not supposed to be deprived of without due process of law and that are nevertheless denied to us, without due process, as a matter of routine.

It would be nice if our families, friends, neighbors, leaders, and other fellow citizens could just get over their prejudices about us. It is really difficult sometimes to see what in the lives we lead should be a source of such interest to so many people. It would be possible to make a list of things we all might like, but there is little consensus among gays and lesbians beyond the basics of equal protection and individual freedom. One thing we agree on is that we want to be left alone, to be free from the constant pressures and prejudices that assail us whether we are out of the closet or not.

At the very least, public institutions should treat gay and lesbian Americans and their lives with the same respect they give heterosexual Americans. The culture has no business promoting heterosexuality at the expense of homosexuality, and if this sounds radical, then ask yourself if you agree that the interests of white Americans or male Americans should not be promoted at the expense of black or female Americans. The same principle of equality is at work in all three cases. People's inclinations, orientation, preference, nature, and private lives should be respected, unless it can be shown that some harm to the public interest would result. This is the principle of equal protection under the law. Although we would like to see reasonable representations of gays and lesbians in the world around us, to have our numbers acknowledged, our needs addressed, our feelings respected, and our accomplishments noted and rewarded, most of us would be happy to gain equal protection and make do without the special attentions society lavishes on heterosexuals. But equal protection is our minimal demand, because the absence of rights is not the same as being let alone. Rights are required to protect individuals from undue interference with their lives by government or majority prejudice. David Mixner said it well in an interview with NBC: "We are going to be free."[1]

Freedom. Gay Americans want freedom.

The right to be left alone to live your life was supposed

to be the point of this constitutional regime. Many Americans share the feeling that our society has forgotten how to mind its own business. Our lives as individuals seem less important than they should be. No class in America is more familiar with the obstacles to individual thriving than lesbians and gay men. When all Americans think about sexual orientation, they should not think about the sex they do not want to have, but whether the sex they do want to have is anyone's business but their own.

For those who believe that meaningful individuality has lost its force in the complex, harried world, gay issues may not resonate. For those who believe that the appropriate response to the modern world is precisely to bolster and reinforce the capacities of the individual, gay rights must resonate powerfully. Heterosexuals who value their own self-knowledge are no more inclined that homosexuals to give in to the moral bullies who would rather yell than reason and who seem to know how everyone ought to live. The point of education, progress, freedom is to liberate internal truths so that our lives may prove more responsive to them.

That was the point of the Declaration of Independence: to stick the principle of individual liberty into the craw of any potential tyranny, whether British, racial, or moral. Gays and lesbians have to struggle very hard to earn our inner freedom. Having done this in significant numbers over the past quarter century, we are determined to secure our civil freedom so that our lives can be as good and safe and decent as anybody else's.

Why should heterosexual Americans care about gay rights? Beyond fairness and decency, what concern is it of theirs? In one of those odd twists of fate that makes history something more or less than a science, the majority of Americans face issues in their lives that gays and lesbians have pioneered. The identification and understanding of the self, apart from family and social and conventional expectations, is what is required for gay people to survive. Such self-understanding is what the reexamination of gender roles, the predominance of serial monogamy or single-parent families, the recasting of families in a more extended and complicated fashion have brought about for people who are not gay. The traditional family is no longer normative. Only one family in five, according to a survey by the Population Reference Bureau, fits the image of a wage-earner father, a wife at home, and two children.[2]

Whether or not one deplores the change in normative family structure, the fact is that more and more Americans have to make personal decisions on the basis of economic, psychological, and sexual realities that force them to re-imagine family rather than to pursue the ideal of family they learned as children. They can no longer depend—nor do many want to depend—on the old, and inherently troubled, ideal of one marriage, one career, one house, and two kids equals one family. The inclusion of gays and lesbians in the model of family, and the model of gay families, are important in a society full of people trying to make their way through life, and to lead good lives, in what have been considered unconventional settings. The great majority of Americans live unconventional lives, if judged by the "traditional" family—which, of course, is not traditional at all but an aberration of the post–World War II era. What gays and lesbians have to teach other Americans is that morality is how you live and how you conduct yourself, not what you happen to be; that family values, like cooperation and respect for the rights of others, have to do with the values inside a family, not whether that family conforms to someone else's idea of what a family should be. What gays and lesbians have to teach other Americans is that an authentic life can be difficult but also satisfying, moving, and rich, and that the kind of openness it can create permits precisely the tolerance for others that must exist in a democratic society.

Individuality requires self-consciousness above all. Making choices for ourselves in public and private life is the challenge of a free democratic society. The pitfalls of this are many; most of the world still falters and reverts to regimes under which people are told what to believe, what to think, and how to act. The totalitarianism of communism is being replaced by the totalitarianism of religion and nationalism throughout the world. The United States has a tradition of freedom to hold on to, but, as always, the challenge freedom presents is uncomfortable for many.

As a people, we are learning about the differences of race, religion, gender, ethnicity that will either divide or unite us. But it is as individuals, which we all have the right and capacity to be, that we make the choices about our personal lives based on inner necessity and principled concern for what is good and what will make us happy. That is, of course, what the "pursuit of happiness" is all about. Those choices are about more than recreation, possessions, and pleasure; they are about identity and private life. Freedom makes one gamble on the private decisions other free citizens make about their lives and the common life. These decisions and choices are the core of freedom, and their protection is the paramount issue of our times.

To acquiesce in the denial to gay and lesbian Americans of equal protection of the law because the idea of their equality worries you or because you don't want to think about homosexuality is bad citizenship. To refuse to recognize yourself in our struggles shows shortsighted self-interest. The forces that seek to oppose our equality are the forces that aim to restrict everyone's right to a truly private life. The more Americans live private lives they have chosen or have hewed out of unexpected circumstance—and that appears to be most of us—the more compelling for everyone is the case for gay rights. We want what you want. We have a right to what you have a right to. The enemies of our right to live freely as individuals are the enemies of your right to live freely as individuals. We all come from your families, and your families cannot survive if we are persecuted. The individualism foreseen by Emerson, the challenge to people to live their lives from the inside out and to make custom and convention respond to the indwelling human truth, has at last become a majority cause; gay rights is the most telling instance of it in our times.

2. THE CASE FOR GAY MARRIAGE

Of the many items we list as objectives of the lesbian and gay rights movement, we have decided to focus on same-sex marriage. We have chosen it in part because it is probably the most controversial item on that list. Even those of our fellow citizens who would support an end to other kinds of discrimination against us balk when the issue of same-sex marriage is raised. For if any one relationship is considered peculiarly heterosexual it is the marital relationship. But we argue that this relationship expresses a human impulse, not a specifically heterosexual one, and that it is as much a creation of law and social policy as of religious belief. We are talking about the civil rather than the religious aspects of marriage. Although some denominations have begun to solemnize same-sex unions, we are not concerned with what religions do or do not do, because that is not a proper sphere in this discussion of constitutional and legal rights. Instead, we are talking again about principles of equal protection and individual liberty.

Marriage is how society recognizes the intimate and lasting bond between two people and, in turn, it has become the cornerstone of the American family. Curiously, the American family as we know it is not "traditional" but innovative. Instead of inherited property or bloodlines or unquestioned patriarchal authority, the American family early on developed the view of marriage as a partnership between two consenting adults, not an agreement on their account by their parents or families. The churches that bless the marriage sacrament took their cue from secular, individualist America and, in general, endorse marriage as something entered into by the participants, if they are of an age to contract, because they choose to make that commitment.

In the United States marriage is understood to be the decision of two people to live together and be a partnership, a unit, a family. Neither family nor church participates in the legal ceremony, and the religious wedding acquires legal force by the power vested in the officiant by the civil society; the religious ceremony confirms the civil arrangement. Marriage is not conditioned on the intention or the capacity to have children. Nothing in marriage, except custom, mandates partners of different genders. For example, John Boswell notes that in ancient Rome "marriages between males and between females were legal and familiar among the upper classes."[3] The institution of marriage in our society appears to be one that encourages monogamy as the basis for stable personal lives and as one aspect of the family. If we think about what marriage is for, it becomes clear that it is for people to find ways to live ordered, shared lives; it is intended to be the stablest possible unit of family life and a stable structure of intimacy.[3]

Marriage is part of the formal and informal network of extended family, kinship, and friendship, and it is acknowledged in law as society's preferred way for consenting adults to connect their lives. Society recognizes that people have the right and the desire to have those connections solemnized according to their own beliefs; thus, religious ceremonies of all sorts, established or homemade, are encouraged as adjuncts to the civil bond. But it is the civil bond that the law acknowledges and that society encourages in all sorts of ways. No wonder many gay and lesbian Americans see marriage as their equal right. Marriage is society's way of making things easier and better for people who want to form permanent relationships, share their lives and property, and form families.

Marriage is not mere form. Society recognizes its importance not only rhetorically but with such benefits as preferential tax treatment, spousal Social Security and veteran's benefits, favorable immigration laws, property and support rights upon divorce, and intestate succession. In addition, according to Alissa Friedman, "both state and federal governments allocate a great many rights on the basis of marital status and have created powerful incentives for an individual to marry. Furthermore, private entities like insurance companies often provide special benefits and lower rates for married couples and legally recognized couples. Restrictions on the right to marry, therefore, affect both associational rights and a variety of societal entitlements."[4]

Marriage is a civil privilege conferred by society. Gays and lesbians are not the first class of Americans denied the right to marry. Slave marriages were not recognized by the law. In the words of a nineteenth-century jurist, "whether [slaves] 'take up' with each other by express permission of their owners or from a mere impulse of nature," their marriages "cannot in the contemplation of the law, make any sort of difference." Well into the twentieth century, miscegenation laws, like Virginia's, not only treated interracial marriages as "absolutely void," but made it a criminal offense to enter such marriages. The punishment in Virginia was "not less than one or more than five years" in prison. The racist beliefs these laws rested on were so commonly held that by 1940, thirty of the forty-eight states banned interracial marriage. In the sphere of marital rights, gays and lesbians are treated as brutally as these earlier Americans were.[5]

It is understandable that certain groups—races, nationalities, religions, regions, classes—would be leery of the results that marriage outside the group would produce. But the legal endorsement of this xenophobic impulse is unacceptable in the United States, as much because of its violation of individual liberty and freedom of choice as because of its obstacles to the intermingling of our varied populace. The government has no right to favor with recognition the bonding rights of some people over others on the basis of race, religion, or sexual orientation. The proscriptions against certain kinds of marriages have no basis outside of convention, and no force when they oppose the stated desire of American citizens to marry.

Gays and lesbians want the right to marry for the same reasons other Americans do: to gain the moral, legal, social, and spiritual benefits conferred on the marrying couple and especially on their family unit. The material benefits of marriage are considerable, but it is the moral benefit that is especially attractive to many couples, including gay and lesbian ones. Marriage is, or can be, a moral commitment that two people make to one another. The marriage vow enshrines love, honor, respect, and mutual support and gives people access to resources and community acknowledgment that serve to strengthen their bond. Brought up and socialized as most Americans are, gays and lesbians also regard the prospect of marriage as reverently and respectfully as heterosexuals do. To mock and deny them is ultimately to mock and deny the institution of marriage. The impulse to marry, among gays, is essentially the same as it is among heterosexuals, and the capacity to do it well is probably the same. The only real difference is in the identity of the people who want to get married.

What is drastically different, of course, is that gay and lesbian unions get none of the support, encouragement, and benefits society regularly gives to heterosexual unions, however ill-advised. Instead, gays and lesbians are reviled for their "inability" to form permanent attachments. Of course, relationships between people that have to remain clandestine or have no foundation in law or social convention are just that much harder to maintain. Gay relationships can succeed, but always against heavy odds, odds not of the participants' making; heterosexual marriages fail all too often in spite of every conceivable social, familial, legal, and moral support.

The journal *Demography* recently published the results of a twenty-three-year study of the relationship of cohabitation to marriage; they suggest "the possibility that cohabitation weakens commitment to marriage as an institution." The authors of the study concluded that living together before marriage may not strengthen marriage; on the contrary, living together before marriage commonly produces "attitudes and values which increase the probability of divorce."[6] These conclusions underscore the particular burdens society places on same-sex couples who try to form and maintain lasting relationships: If the chosen cohabitation of heterosexuals weakens their bonds, how could it not weaken the relationships of same-sex couples who not only *may not* marry but in addition struggle against the stereotype that their relationships must inevitably dissolve? If, as the *Demography* study indicates, marriage is a key ingredient in the longevity and solidity of intimate relationships, then denial of that most important advantage to one class of citizens on account of sexual orientation is cruelly unfair.

One of the ironies of our situation is that the American marriage that is so celebrated actually borrows from the historical character of gay relationships to describe itself. Far from being unnatural, gay and lesbian ways of living have played important roles in every human society. One almost universal function of those relationships has been to pioneer the more equal relations between the sexes. Long-standing relationships between men and between women are well known to history. Antiquity celebrated the bonds of friendship and loyalty between men, bonds that scholars tell us commonly included the sexual. The relationships among Greek soldiers and philosophers, which have played so critical a role in the traditional Western understanding of noble human relations (including the cohesion of the military unit), were modeled on love between men that regularly included sex.

The lifelong partnerships between middle-class or upper-class women in American history—the famous "Boston marriages"—also influenced decisively the understanding of marriage that American women derived from their colleges and their genteel upbringings. Female friendships played a critical role in the creation of the American institution of marriage as a partnership within which the woman was not owned but respected, not a human beast of burden and procreation but an equal source of authority and values for the family that marriage creates. When the modern American marriage departed from the model of female servitude and adopted the ideal of partnership between husband and wife, so lately celebrated by Marilyn Quayle and Barbara Bush, it drew on the model of respectful and loving partnerships between women and between men as a way of teaching men to respect women as they respect men, women to partner with men as they had with women.

The distinctive quality of modern American marriage and family is the equal and respectful, relations between husband and wife as partners, friends, and co-parents, in the place of the economic, procreative, and kinship unit of traditional societies. Men and women are learning to treat one another as they more habitually treat favored members of their own gender—with confidence, trust, equality, respect, and sensitivity. Gays and lesbians are as capable of forming such relationships and making them work as heterosexual men and women are.

Gays and lesbians seek the legitimacy heterosexual marriages have that consecrates and supports the married lives of heterosexuals and that borrows so much from homosexual lives. Gays and lesbians have intimate associations, but do not enjoy the same rights as other Americans to have those associations protected and rewarded by material benefits or moral sanctions. Of course, many gays and lesbians, like many heterosexuals, may not want marriage and the ways in which it brings society into personal arrangements. We do not advocate that anyone choose to be married; we insist, however, on the equal right of gays and lesbians to marry if they choose.

Two main obstacles appear to gay marriage: legal definitions of marriage and the claim that marriage is chiefly for procreation or child-rearing. The legal argument boils down to the following: Marriage is a union of man and woman because it's always been that way. The civil law that governs marriage has its roots in ecclesiastical law, which reflects the biblical proscription of homosexuality. The statutes say that marriage is the union of man and woman, so that is what marriage must be. Moreover, marriage, it is sometimes argued, is instituted for the purpose of procreation. This circular and mindless excuse for judicial reasoning is usually accompanied by sarcasm, disbelief, and the sound effects of incredulity at the thought of gay or lesbian marriage.[7]

In *Singer v. Hara,* a decision from Washington state, the plaintiffs, two men who wished to marry, argued that the state's equal rights amendment forbidding gender discrimination made it unconstitutional for same-sex couples to be prohibited from marrying. The state's chief judge made short work of this argument: "Appellants are not being denied entry into the marriage relationship because of their sex; rather, they are being denied entry into the marriage relationship because of the recognized definition of that relationship as one which may be entered into only by two persons of the opposite sex."[8] In other words, "You can't be married because marriage means two people of the opposite sex."

This is what is called in the law ipse dixit reasoning: "It's so because I say it's so." But undeniably, it expresses a deeply and commonly held belief among heterosexual Americans. It is worth remembering, however, that even though marriage is traditionally defined as a legal union between a man and a woman, the union itself is not so defined. Same-sex unions have an ancient and honorable tradition, celebrated in literature, philosophy, history, and religion. Just as the union between men and women may include sexual relations but is more than a sexual relationship, so, too, the union between men and men or women and women may include sexual relationships but means much more. No one has a monopoly on love, either the desire to love or to be loved, or the desire to make of that love a life-long bond not only acknowledged and honored by the participants but also by the community they live in. The only reason—*the only reason*—that marriage is denied to us is to promote heterosexuality. Of course, there are objections that the society would be extending the material benefits of marriage to a whole new class of people, but who do you think presently supports those benefits and gets nothing in return? Gay and lesbian taxpayers, of course. We do not mean to denigrate heterosexual marriage or heterosexuality; what we are saying is that under our constitutional system no status can be promoted at the expense of another.

Even if we accept parenting as one important reason for the institution of marriage, shifting the model of marriage to include common if untraditional parenting units makes sense. Whatever was the case in the past, it is now common for gays and lesbians to be parents, not just to have fathered and borne children in heterosexual unions, but to be raising children as open gays and lesbians. In a survey of gay couples, Mary Mendola looked at gays and lesbians involved in a "gay marriage relationship," as she put it. She found that a quarter of the women and 17 percent of the men reported that they or their partners had children. Nearly 60 percent of the women reported that their children lived with them and their partners most of the time, while 39 percent reported that their children regularly visited. While only 3 percent of the men reported that their children lived with them and their partners, 53 percent reported that their children regularly visited them.[9] Mendola's report is a dozen years old; if anything the numbers have probably increased as more gays and lesbians are producing children by using artificial insemination (the so-called gayby boom) or adopting them or winning custody of them. If society is serious in its claim that marriage produces the best environment for raising children, then marriage must be extended to gays and lesbians who, in increasing numbers, are becoming parents.

Moreover, the studies available on gay parenting demonstrate that gays and lesbians make good parents; the children of gay families appear to do as well as the children of heterosexual ones.[10] If, as it is sometimes argued, these children face difficulties among their peers because of negative attitudes toward homosexuality, the clear solution is to change those attitudes through education. Allowing same-sex marriage would be an important part of that change and would also promote family stability. If, in fact, that kind of stability is one of the reasons that marriage exists, it makes no sense to promote it in some families but not others by restricting marriage to heterosexuals.

Opponents of gay marriage finally arrive at the bedrock of their argument when they assert that allowing gays and lesbians to marry would encourage illegal sexual activity in the face of sodomy laws. The argument, which relies heavily on the Supreme Court's decision in *Bowers v. Hardwick,* is as follows: If states can criminalize same-sex sexual activity and this, in turn, implies a moral judgment against that activity (even in places where there are no sodomy laws), then allowing gays and lesbians to marry is contrary to acceptable morality. Of course, the whole point of gay and lesbian activism is to expose the underlying premise of immorality for the bigotry it is. Making an act illegal doesn't mean the act is inherently criminal.

On the issue of homosexuality, the culture is in a period of flux and there is no longer unanimity that reducing the incidence of homosexuality activity is an acceptable social goal. In any event, while sodomy laws may have limited the possibilities for gay and lesbian sexual activity, there is no evidence that it reduced the numbers of gays and lesbians. Conversely, the quarter century of gay and lesbian political activism and openness has not resulted in a dramatic increase in the homosexual population (although it has dramatically increased the awareness of homosexuality and has also increased the numbers of lesbians and gay living openly). This points to the conclusion that this population is relatively stable and will always be a minority. Thus, punitive laws accomplish nothing but to intimidate a class of American citizens and deny them their constitutional rights. Denying gays and lesbian marriage will not eliminate gay and lesbian relationships; it will just make those relationships harder to sustain. If creating unnecessary suffering in the cause of popular prejudice is a permissible goal of legislation, then not only gay Americans are in for a bad time of it.

If arguments against gay marriage rest on the shifting sands of social habit, arguments for gay marriage rest on the understanding of marriage as a creation of civil law, and civil law is not immutable. The civil law of marriage has changed so much over history that one can make the argument that marriage is a gauge of the changing character of human relations and social and religious institutions over time. In his essay "Regulating the American Family," Steven Mintz writes that "with the triumph of individualistic, egalitarian and contractual values, the law tends to reinforce broader individualistic and therapeutic currents in the culture, stressing self-fulfillment and individual happiness as the ultimate social values. As a result, we have almost precisely inverted the values and mode of discourse of our Puritan forefathers." And, as historian David Stannard observes in his article "Changes in the American Family: Fiction and Reality," our culture is experiencing a crisis in family, a crisis "founded on our inability or unwillingness to allow our fictions to catch up with our realities and our realities to catch up with our fictions."[11]

The religious right and some courts may not like it, but significant numbers of Americans who are also gay and lesbian meet all but one of the criteria for marriage. They are citizens, parents, taxpayers, upstanding people of all creeds, colors, habits, and views, scattered across the religious, political, social, racial, and ethnic divisions of our complex society. They are missing only heterosexuality as a qualification for marriage. All that stands between them and the proper application of equal protection is the insistence on privileging heterosexuality for its own sake.

We can only speculate about the effects of the legalization of gay marriage on the society at large. It could introduce new stability and security into the lives of millions of Americans who, but for their sexual orientation, resemble their fellow citizens in their aspirations and beliefs. It would place on the shoulders of gays and lesbians the moral responsibility for their own lives. You can't, after all, take responsibility for what you are denied access to, and responsibility is a gift of freedom. Gay marriage might just reinfuse the beleaguered institutions of marriage and family with fresh enthusiasm, reality and life, restoring them to their proper character as a serious and important means for humans to achieve intimacy, stability, and shelter from the storms of life.

In any case, far from harming heterosexuals, gay marriage would give family-inclined gay men and lesbians the chance to fulfill this aspiration in conformity with their own natures.

The legitimacy of gay marriage would save lives by creating the kind of respect for gays and lesbians that will work as a counterweight to bigotry and bashing. Gay marriage would also deal a decisive blow to the religious terrorism and evangelical imperialism that would use fear of gay and lesbian rights to impose an illicit, ill-considered, and unconstitutional authority over everyone. The key to equal protection of the laws is the recognition of the individual's rights, and crucial to those rights is the right of intimate association, family-making, and inevitably, therefore, marriage.

While we were writing this book, support for our argument that denying lesbians and gay men the right to marry violates equal protection came from an unexpected quarter. In *Baehr v. Lewin,* the Supreme Court of Hawaii reversed the decision of a lower court that had dismissed a lawsuit brought by gay and lesbian couples challenging the constitutionality of Hawaii's marriage statutes, which barred same-sex couples from marrying. The case now returns to the lower court for trial, but the Hawaii Supreme Court's opinion was a clear signal to the trial court that the statute is unconstitutional on equal protection grounds.

The court began its discussion of the plaintiff's equal protection claim by observing that the "power to regulate marriage is a sovereign function reserved exclusively for the respective states." That power, the court said, includes "the power to regulate the marriage relation . . . to determine the requisites of a valid marriage contract and to control the qualifications of the contracting parties." The court catalogued the benefits denied to same-sex couples as a consequence of not being able to marry: income tax advantages, public assistance to families, community property and support rights, the right of spousal support, the right to enter into premarital agreements, to a change of name, the spousal privilege and confidential-marital-communication exception when giving testimony, and the right to bring a wrongful-death action upon the negligent death of a spouse.[12]

After this review, the court concluded that the state may deny the right to marry "only for compelling reasons." It found no such reason for the denial to same-sex couples of the right to marry. Faced with the state's argument that the right to marry persons of the same sex does not exist because marriage is a "special relationship" between a man and a woman, the court commented, "We believe [the] argument to be circular and unpersuasive." Addressing an old decision of the Virginia Supreme Court upholding the ban on inter-racial marriage on the grounds that offended it Divine Providence, the court observed: "With all due respect to the Virginia Courts of a bygone era, we do not believe that trial courts are the ultimate authorities on the subject of Divine Will, and . . . Constitutional law may mandate, like it or not, that customs change with an evolving social order." Having analyzed *Singer v. Hara,* the Washington case we discussed above, the court dismissed it as an "exercise in tortured and confusing sophistry."[13]

Coming to its own view of the equal protection argument, the Hawaii court declared that sex-based discrimination is presumptively unconstitutional and that the marriage statute could only be upheld if there were compelling state interests in retaining it. The court left open the possibility that the state could show such compelling interest, so it is not settled whether Hawaii will become the first state to permit same-sex marriages. With this decision, however, the Hawaiian Supreme Court does become the first American court to acknowledge that marriage is not the creation of someone's God, but of the state, and that denial of the right to marry cannot be justified by theological argument or appeals to Divine Providence. Like all other incidents of citizenship, the right to marry must be determined in the light of the constitutional guarantee of equal protection.[14]

3. WHAT WE WANT

What do gays and lesbians want? What does any person want? Enough to live; basic protections; love, family, freedom. Beyond the basics, in the case of gays and lesbians, would be equal protection of the law, representation along with taxation. And what lies beyond that, it is the individual's place to say. We do not think there is a shared agenda among gays and lesbians that goes much beyond equality and freedom. But there are some other things that we imagine as human counterparts to legal protections.

It would be wonderful if families could see in their children the full range of the affectional possibilities that life in fact holds out. If girlish boys and boyish girls, who do not constitute the full range of homosexuality but who are often the ones targeted, could receive encouragement and praise and the love they deserve instead of derision, intimidation, and disappointment, their lives would be much improved. And it would improve the quality of the culture if these children could grow into adults who, because they were loved and valued, made rich contributions to the culture instead of expending that energy on overcoming the wounds that were inflicted on them.

It would also be wonderful if friends and colleagues of gay people would be as interested in their lives as they are in their company and counsel, if the walls came down and revealed each other's essential humanity. And it would be wonderful to see gay and lesbian judges, mayors, kindergarten teachers, construction workers, actors, fathers, brothers, mothers, sisters, musicians and clerics, all of them acknowledged and honored. In this utopia, little would appear changed, but there would be an addition rather than a diminution of freedom and well-being. But this is not a utopian book. What we have written about, what gays and lesbians want, is our constitutional rights.

We also think gay people want their fellow Americans to join with them in this cause as we have always joined with our families and friends in other causes. We hope the readers of this book will recognize in the demand of gays and lesbians for equality and freedom, the echoes of the defining promise of our liberal democracy. To us, the issue is so clearly and starkly drawn that it is sometimes hard to figure out what the hesitation is on the part of others. On the one side are ranged people who not only believe that homosexuality is a sin, but that the Constitution of the United States is supposed to endorse their views by denying legal protections to gays and lesbians. On the other side are gay and lesbian Americans who do not understand why their lives and the choices they make are anybody's business but their own. They do not understand why what they are by nature and in their private lives should make them ineligible for rights as citizens, which they also are. What gay Americans want is what all Americans are supposed to have. It's that simple.

Created Equal

$\mathbf{M}$OST LESBIANS AND gay men are ordinary human beings who want from life the things most other people want: economic security, comfortable shelter, enough to eat, safe streets, a place to worship God, the love of family and friends, and most of all, to love and be loved. Most of them never wanted to be outlaws or to be faced with the choice of being true to themselves or lying about their lives in order to get by without being scorned, rejected, or physically attacked. They do not relish having to make public disclosures of private matters simply to win the right of privacy that everybody else takes for granted.

Most gay men and lesbians would probably not have made the revolution that began with the homophile movement in the early 1950s, passed through the firestorm of Stonewall in 1969, and has become the lesbian and gay movement of our time. That work took eccentric daredevils cut from heroic cloth. But having had the taste of freedom and self-respect that history has given them collectively and that coming out has given them individually, lesbians and gay men of all sorts, from all regions, from every racial and ethnic group, from every class, have realized that the freedoms America promises, most of all the freedom to live an ordinary life, are theirs by constitutional right. Having felt the stirrings of freedom and self-respect, lesbian and gay Americans have been radicalized by the traditional American values of individual liberty that our constitutional regime, however imperfectly, enshrines.

Speaking now for ourselves, we wish that we had not believed it was necessary to write this book, and to think about the issues we have raised in it, because it has been painful and difficult for us to confront the fear and the hatred that many of our fellow citizens not only bear toward us but freely express in the street, from the pulpits, in the halls of Congress, and in the chambers of the Supreme Court. It has been painful and difficult also to craft arguments on which so much seems to us to be riding. We have written this book because we want things to happen and people to change and our readers to act and think differently than we imagine they have.

But we have been heartened throughout, as have many of our fellow gays and lesbians, by the fact that we live in a country that has allowed us to state our case. We, like you, were schoolchildren when we first studied the words of Jefferson and the other American founders who expressed their often narrow interests in binding language of such generous, universal liberation. They raised an inspiring standard for their new country to aspire to and for its unjustly treated people to hold it to.

It took us a long time, as it did many other homosexuals, to recognize the connection between the founders' actions and the situation of our own lives. But in time we came to understand that the phrase "life, liberty and the pursuit of happiness" meant our lives, and our liberty, and the pursuit of our happiness. These are not words to be examined on old parchment by dim light in a marble corridor, or to be carved in stone. They are blood and bone, heart, mind, and soul. The founders had to ask themselves, "Why live if not as free men?" We, and every other gay man and woman, have had to ask the same thing of ourselves. Now we ask our fellow citizens why and by what right should we be expected to live without freedom and equality.

America tells us that citizens of this country possess the inalienable right of freedom, and that government exists for no higher purpose than to protect the exercise of that freedom. America promises that the law shall be applied equally to all of us, regardless of our differences and *especially* if those differences incite prejudice in others. America tells us that the Constitution is a living thing, a framework that bends to accommodate and protect the freedom of every group of Americans that seeks its protections, whether or not the founders could have envisioned their specific claim. America guarantees that we shall be free to worship God in the manner of our choosing, but that no other person's God will dictate how we are to live our own lives. Does America stop meaning all this when it comes to lesbians and gay men? America can only answer through the voices of its citizens, through you.

We have believed what America promised—and in this we differ from many other gay people, whose bitter skepticism we acknowledge and understand and have sometimes shared. We know, however, that were change as simple as our belief, there would be no need to write this book. The question is about your beliefs. Do you believe that American citizens who are gay and lesbian deserve the same protections as you do, as every other American citizen does? We know you hesitate in answering that question, and we know why. Your imagination is filled with the frightening specters of queers, dykes, homos, faggots, child molesters, leathermen, diesels, drag queens, and perverts. When you hear the words "homosexual," "gay," and "lesbian," you think of strange people having weird sex: cocksuckers, men who take it up the ass, women with strap-on dildos, fistfuckers, sadists, masochists, and whatever other words you know or images you have in your mind that described what you believe to be the sexual practices of gay people.

When we think of the words "homosexual," "gay," and "lesbian" we see ourselves standing up for ourselves and our kind, unashamed. We also see the faces of beloved friends, of doctors, lawyers, teachers, writers, artists, students, psychologists, librarians, gardeners, politicians, workers, and businesspeople. They have names. They have families. They have lives. Many have children. Too many still struggle with the pain of having grown up, as we did, lonely and shamed in their identity. Some have lovers, often of many years' standing, and some do not. Too many have AIDS. Too many have died. Some are married, or have been married, to people of the opposite sex. But they are, as Christopher Isherwood put it, *our kind.*

We do not concern ourselves with their sex lives any more than they concern themselves with ours, any more than any of us concern ourselves with the sex lives of our heterosexual friends or family members, because other people's sex lives are none of our business and they are none of yours. We have said it probably a dozen times in this book, and we will say it again: Homosexuality is not exclusively about sex any more than heterosexuality is.

What does the opposition to gay and lesbian equality come down to? Simply this: unfamiliarity. The word "familiar" derives from the Latin for "family," and those with whom we are familiar are, in some extended sense, our family. Those with whom we are unfamiliar we do not think of in the same way. And that makes it easy for us to regard these people with curiosity and trepidation. Curiosity can be satisfied and trepidation can be overcome, but it requires effort on the part of everyone.

The reason that gays and lesbians urge their closeted friends to come out is that by so doing we take steps toward you, our fellow citizens; democracy requires this of us. But you must also take some steps toward us, because democracy requires it of you. We do not mean, necessarily, that you have to befriend your neighborhood homosexual, that household of two women just down the street, or the single man in the next apartment. Even from a distance, you can recognize that these people are, in fact, people in the process of living their lives. If you can connect that observation to the further observation that they are homosexual, then you have come as far as you must to acknowledge that they are entitled to their lives and property just as you are. Even by reading this book and thinking about what we have said, you can begin to bridge that distance, and begin to understand what gay and lesbian rights is all about.

We want you to do this because we know that once you attach a face and a life to the word "homosexual," it will be harder for you to hang on to your old, pejorative habits of thinking. And if you actually befriend a gay person, then it will be nearly impossible for you to hang on to prejudice. That is what we want. That's our "homosexual agenda." It is precisely the opposite of the religious right, which wants to keep gays closeted so that you can go on believing that we are bizarre or sick or sinful. You ought to be suspicious of people who want to keep you in ignorance, and you ought to ask why. Whose interests does it serve to keep you ignorant of the real lives of gay people? Your own?

You may think that you neither want nor need to know about gays and lesbians, so what does it matter if you are kept in ignorance. But think of it this way: Dividing and conquering is a political tactic first learned in the schoolyard. If a schoolyard bully picks on one kid, and no one stands up for that kid, what's to the prevent the bully from picking on you as his next target? You watch the sissy kid being pummeled and your first response is relief that it wasn't you. Then, later, because you feel some guilt at doing nothing, you tell yourself that no one liked that kid anyway, so he probably deserved the beating. The thought is comforting because you know that you haven't done anything to deserve a beating. But this is an illusion. Bullies find reasons to beat people up because beating people up is what bullies do.

So, you think, I'm not a homosexual, and no one likes homosexuals anyway, so who cares if they get beat up? But maybe you live with someone to whom you're not married, or maybe you're a single parent and your child is in day care so you can earn a living. Maybe you're a woman who once had an abortion or maybe you're just someone who believes that women have the right to choose abortion. Maybe you're a Jew, or a Mormon, or an Episcopalian and you take your religious observance seriously. Maybe you're African-American and all too aware of the surviving racial discrimination in this society. Maybe you're an artist of some kind, a painter or novelist or photographer or an actor or a filmmaker, and your artistic vision takes into account the moral and sexual lives of your subjects. Maybe you are someone who likes to go to galleries, the movies, or the theater, or even likes to catch a glimpse of human variety on your TV set. The freedoms you take for granted are part and parcel of the freedom that must be restricted if the current campaign against lesbian and gay equality is successful. The restrictionists cannot get to us without doing harm to your freedom. When they finish with us, they will find reason to come after you. And they will say that you have given them reason.

You may think we exaggerate the threat to individual liberty posed by the religious right and its political allies. It is true that they have not succeeded in their goal of gaining national political power—yet—but this is their aim; they are well financed, well led, and well organized, and their ideology is based on the rejection of individualism and cultural pluralism. The only way to defeat a bully is for all of his potential victims to make common cause against him. What we have been asking in this book is that you begin examining the arguments in favor of gay and lesbian equality and holding them up against the arguments advanced by our opponents. You may agree that our arguments are meritorious but balk at the prospect of their enactment. *Gay marriage?* Let us then restate those arguments.

Discrimination against homosexuality and against lesbian and gay individuals is founded in the fact that we are in a sexual minority. The very intimate nature of sexual orientation and the pervasiveness of cultural prejudice against gays and lesbians makes it easy for feelings of prejudice to be stirred up against gays. The stereotypes of lesbians and gays that support this prejudice are simply not true. The claim that homosexuality is specially singled out by the Judeo-Christian God for opprobrium is, at best, disputed. The implication that the government should enact this claim is not only unconstitutional but problematic for heterosexuals who trespass against undisputed elements of that God's code; think about adultery, for instance, or the implications of restricting sex not intended for procreation.

The anti-gay activists' interpretation of the Constitution is dangerous to everybody's First Amendment liberties. Our opponents claim that homosexuality disqualifies an American from equal citizenship because they believe, as is their right, that to be gay or lesbian is immoral. They claim that as part of their freedom of religion the Constitution permits them to impose the standard of morality derived from their own religious views. This claim is disingenuous. Their real belief is that they must impose their own agenda on the body politic. This not the first time a sectarian group has tried to use freedom to impose its restrictionist views, nor will it be the last. That is why we have the First Amendment.

The refusal of the courts to extend privacy rights and equal protection of the laws to gay and lesbian Americans is based on prejudice. An examination of the decisions shows prejudice and mockery where argument ought to be. The refusal of local, state, and federal governments to protect their gay and lesbian citizens—indeed, their continuing harassment of and discrimination against them—is based on the same morass of ill-reasoned prejudice. Even the majority, whether acting as a voting public as in Colorado or through the organs of popular government, has not the authority to deprive minorities of their constitutional rights.

The continuing invisibility of gays and lesbians in the culture and its historical and contemporary representations contributes to our oppression. The movement against homosexuals only barely conceals the real agenda of the anti-gay activists: the replacement of individual freedom, about which they have always been uneasy, with their own strict and reactionary views of society and family life. The campaign against gays is really a campaign against modern American society and against the freer women and men who populate and struggle in it. Gay rights attempts to structure that freedom with fairness so that we can get on with the business of building real and stable lives for all the different kinds of people and families inhabiting this country.

Gays and lesbians participate in this society by, as President Clinton likes to say, working hard and playing by the rules. It is not only your labor and taxes but ours that support the social system from which you benefit in ways that we do not. This situation presents a simple matter of fairness. Marriage is a legal status that entitles those who enter into it benefits ranging from health insurance coverage to some tax breaks. It is not fair to deny those benefits to gays and lesbians by enacting laws that prevent us from obtaining them when we contribute to the system that makes those benefits possible. Fairness is what this is about—not the sanctity of marriage or the "promotion" of homosexuality, but fairness.

You may think that all of this would mean, ultimately, that homosexual "lifestyles" will be the equivalent of heterosexual "lifestyles." You would be right. The title of this book, *Created Equal*, implies that gays and lesbians deserve to be on an equal footing with heterosexuals in the realm of citizenship. We are arguing for equality—not for some slice of the pie, but for equal access to it. If this sounds radical to you, it is only because you are accustomed, in a hundred different ways, of thinking that homosexuals are your inferiors. Perhaps the primary purpose of this book has been to show you that this way of thinking rests upon false beliefs and stereotypes perpetuated about gays and lesbians. Putting those aside, there is no rational argument to justify the subjection of gay people.

It all comes down to this: Are people equal in this society by virtue of their citizenship, or not? If the answer is no, then we will be saying that equality does not exist in America anymore but has been replaced with tiers of citizenship, and that what tier you occupy depends on whether people like you or not. And if we accept this, then we will have repudiated the constitutional principles of liberty and equality upon which America was founded and which have been its historic challenge to the world. If we believed that people were really willing to accept our disenfranchisement after learning the true facts of our case, we would not have written this book. We believe that you will join our cause because it is your cause, too, the cause of individual liberty and human equality.

Notes

Preface

1. John Stuart Mill, "The Subjection of Women," in *John Stuart Mill: Three Essays* (New York: Oxford University Press, 1975), p. 427.
2. Ibid.
3. James Baldwin, *The Fire Next Time* (New York: Laurel, 1988), pp. 18, 20.

Chapter 1: The Ick Factor

1. Hate crime statistics: *USA Today*, March 30, 1992; news release of the Anti-Violence Project of the Los Angeles Gay and Lesbian Community Services Center, March 11, 1993. For an example of how antigay extremists try to exclude gay-bashing from the category of hate crimes, see Marian Wallace, "Junior Scholastic Pushes Gay Agenda," in *Family Voice*, May 1993 (vol. 15, no. 5), p. 29.
2. *U.S. News and World Report*, July 5, 1993, p. 42.
3. *The New York Times*, August 15, 1993, and *Los Angeles Times*, August 16, 1993.
4. See especially David Brion Davis, *From Homicide to Slavery: Studies in American Culture* (New York: Oxford University Press, 1986), pp. 127–86. Richard Hofstadter, *The Paranoid Style in American Politics* (New York: Vintage, 1967).
5. *Casey v. Planned Parenthood of Southeastern Pennsylvania* (1992), 120 L.Ed.2d 674, 698.

6. Bureau of Justice Statistics, *Sourcebook of Criminal Justice Statistics* (Washington, D.C.: Department of Justice, 1992), p. 266.

7. "American ladies will not be slaves"; in Sara Evans, *Born for Liberty: A History of Women in America* (New York: Free Press, 1989), p. 99.

8. *Loving v. Virginia* (1966), 388 US 1, 3.

9. Alice Miller, *For Your Own Good: Hidden Cruelty in Child Rearing and the Roots of Violence* (New York: Farrar, Straus, Giroux, 1989), p. 85.

Chapter 2: Big Lies, Hard Truths

1. John D'Emilio, *Sexual Politics, Sexual Communities* (Chicago: University of Chicago Press, 1983), p. 57.

2. *Newsweek,* September 14, 1992, p. 36.

3. *U.S. News & World Report,* July 5, 1992, p. 42.

4. Guy Hocquenghem, *Homosexual Desire* (London: Allison and Busby, 1978), p. 41; *The New York Times,* August 26, 1992; interview with Scott Valentine, *The Advocate,* October 20, 1992, p. 65.

5. *Jacobson v. Jacobson* (1981), 314 N.W.2d 78, 81.

6. D'Emilio, op. cit., p. 13.

7. *Citizens for Responsible Behavior v. Superior Court* (1991) 1 Cal.App.4th 1013, 1037.

8. Anita Bryant quoted in Lillian Faderman, *Odd Girls and Twilight Lovers* (New York: Columbia University Press, 1991), pp. 333–34, 35; p. 136.

9. Andrea Dworkin, *Intercourse* (New York: The Free Press, 1987), p. 184.

10. For discussions of the importance of sexual definitions in the perpetuation of American racial domination see: Joel Williamson, *A Rape for Order: Black-White Relations in the American South Since Emancipation* (New York: Oxford University Press, 1986) and Dolores Janiewski, *Sisterhood Denied: Race, Gender and Class in a New South Community* (Philadelphia: Temple University Press, 1985), pp. 38–40.

11. Barry D. Adam, *The Survival of Domination: Inferiorization and Everyday Life* (New York: Elsevier New Holland, 1973), p. 45; Adolf Hitler, *Mein Kampf,* English translation (New York: Stackpole Sons, 1939), p. 316, quoted in *The Advocate,* April 7, 1992, p. 27.

12. See comparative female/male rape statistics: Bureau of Justice Statistics, *Sourcebook of Criminal Justice Statistics* (Washington, D.C.: Department of Justice, 1992), p. 266.

13. Michel Foucault, *The History of Sexuality: An Introduction* (New York: Vintage, 1978), p. 53; Hocquenghem, op. cit., p. 59; Faderman, op. cit., p. 59.

14. Jonathan Ned Katz, *Gay American History* (New York: Meridian, 1972) pp. 154–55, 165–67, 181–82; Thomas Moore quoted in ibid., p. 174.

15. Anthony Pietropinto and Jacqueline Simenauer, *Beyond the Male Myth* (New York: Times Books, 1971), p. 62; "ill primarily in terms . . . ": quoted in Sylvia Law, "Homosexuality and the Social Meaning of Gender," *Wisconsin Law Review*, 1988, p. 205, n. 92 (our emphasis).

16. Alfred Kinsey, *Sexual Behavior in the Human Male* (Philadelphia: W. B. Saunders, 1948), p. 639. See also Paul H. Gebhard "Kinsey's Famous Figure" in University of Indiana Alumni Bulletin September/October 1993, p. 64, which concludes, "In summary, Kinsey's two famous figures, despite their methodological flaws, are not bad estimates of reality and can be used for practical purposes in determining social policy. . . . "

17. *Bradwell v. Illinois* (1872) 83 U.S. 130, 141 (concurring opinion, Bradley, J.).

18. Dan Coats, "Clinton's Big Mistake," *The New York Times,* January 30, 1993.

19. Georgia doctor quoted in Katz, op. cit., p. 165; *The Advocate,* June 30, 1992, p. 63.

20. St. Thomas Aquinas quoted in Edward Batchelor, Jr., ed., *Homosexuality and Ethics* (New York: Pilgrim Press, 1981), pp. 40; Barry Adam, op. cit., p. 34.

21. Pat Buchanan quoted in *The New York Times*, March 1, 1992; *Bowers v. Hardwick* (1986), 478 U.S. 186.

22. *The Advocate,* June 30, 1992, pp. 56–58; *The New York Times,* March 18, 1992.

23. Michael Bronski, *Culture Clash: The Making of a Gay Sensibility* (Boston: South End Press, 1984), p. 18; Larry Kramer, *Reports from the Holocaust* (New York: St. Martin's Press, 1989), pp. 178–79.

24. *Newsweek,* September 14, 1992, p. 36; *Los Angeles Times,* January 11, 1993, p. 25.

25. *The New York Times,* May 23, 1993; May 6, 1993.

26. J. Bradley and N. O'Bolensky, eds. *Planning to Live: Evaluating and Treating Suicidal Teens in Community Settings* (Tulsa: National Resource Center, University of Oklahoma, 1990), pp. 297–316; P. Gibson, "Gay Male and Lesbian Youth Suicide," in *Report of the Secretary's Task Force on Youth Suicide, Vol. 3: Prevention and Intervention in Youth Suicide* (Rockville, Md.: U.S. Department of Health and Human Services, 1989); "Gay Youth Six Times More Likely to Commit Suicide," *Washington Blade,* May 16, 1986; *People v. Robert Rosenkrantz* (1988) 198 Cal.App.3d 1187.

27. Christopher Isherwood, *A Single Man* (New York: Noonday Press, 1964), p. 72.

28. Gershon Kaufman, *The Psychology of Shame* (Cambridge, Mass.: Springer Publishing Co., 1989), p. 17.

29. Camille Paglia interview in *The Advocate,* February 11, 1992, p. 74.

30. Jane Goldman, "Coming Out Strong," *California Lawyer,* September 1992, p. 32.

Chapter 3: How Prejudice Works

1. *Bowers v. Hardwick* (1986), 478 U.S. 186.

2. *Thornburg v. American College of Obst. & Gyn.* (1985), 476 U.S. 747, 777, n. 5.

3. *Hardwick v. Bowers* (11th Cir. 1985) 760 F.2d 1202, 1211, 1212.

4. *Griswold v. Connecticut* (1965), 381 U.S. 479, 485–86; *Eisenstadt v. Baird* (1972), 405 U.S. 438, 453; *Roe v. Wade* (1972), 410 U.S. 113, 136.

5. *Casey v. Planned Parenthood* (1992) 120 L.Ed.2d 674, 698; id. 697.

6. Id 698.

7. *Bowers v. Hardwick,* supra, 478 U.S. 186, 190, 192, 194, 196, 196.

8. *Casey v. Planned Parenthood,* supra, 120 L.Ed.2d, 674, 692. 192.

9. Oliver Wendell Holmes, "The Path of the Law," *Harvard Law Review* 1897, p. 469.

10. *Bowers v. Hardwick,* 478 U.S. 186, 190; *Casey v. Planned Parenthood* 120 L.Ed. 674, 697.

11. *Bowers v. Hardwick,* 478 U.S. 186, 196; *Casey v. Planned Parenthood,* 120 L.Ed. 674, 697.

12. *Commonwealth of Kentucky v. Wasson* (Ky. 1992), 842 S.W.2d 487, 502 (Combs, J., concurring).

13. *Bowers v. Hardwick,* 478 U.S. 186, 213–14 (Blackmun, J., dissenting).

14. *Evans v. Romer* (1993) 854 P.2d 1270.

15. *United States v. Carolene Products* (1938) 304 U.S. 144, 152–53, n. 4.

16. *Watkins v. U.S. Army* (9th Cir. 1988) 847 F.2d 1429, 1450.

17. *Evans v. Romer,* supra, 854 P.2d 1270, 1282–85.

18. See, e.g., 21 Vermont Statutes Annotated 495 [prohibiting employment discrimination on basis of sexual orientation]; Massachussetts General Laws Annotated, Ch. 151B, subdivision (1) [employment discrimination] and subdivision (6) [housing].

Chapter 4: "God Hates Fags"

1. *The Reformer,* vol. 9, no. 4 (July/August 1993), p. 3; *Newsweek,* September 14, 1992, p. 36.

2. Pat Robertson, *Answer to 200 of Life's Most Probing Questions* (Nashville: Thomas Nelson, 1984), p. 162; Garry Wills, *Under God* (New York: Simon & Schuster, 1990), pp. 357, 359.

3. Quoted in Wills, op. cit., pp. 358, 359.

4. American Baptist Church statement quoted in *The Advocate,* April 7, 1992, p. 20.

5. Chris Glaser, *Come Home* (San Francisco: HarperCollins, 1990), pp. 101–102, 130–31.

6. John P. McNeill, *The Church and the Homosexual* (Kansas City, Kans.: Sneed, Andrews and McMeel, 1976), p. 17.

7. Reverend Bailey Smith quoted in Frances Fitzgerald, *Cities on a Hill* (New York: Simon & Schuster, 1986), p. 17; Robertson, op. cit., pp. 137–38.

8. James Dobson and Gary Bauer, *Children at Risk* (Dallas: World Publishing, 1990), p. 224.

9. Fitzgerald, op. cit., p. 126.

10. Quoted in ibid., p. 129.

11. Dobson and Bauer, op. cit., p. 3.

12. Robertson, op. cit., p. 239; Charles Colson, *Against the Night* (Ann Arbor, Mich.: Servant Publications, 1989), p. 69; Edward Hindson quoted in Fitzgerald, op. cit., p. 140.

13. Robertson, op. cit., p. 171; Fitzgerald, op. cit., p. 190.

14. Jerry Falwell, *Strength for the Journey,* p. 337.

15. *Salt,* vol. 3, no. 3 (1993), p. 1; *The Reformer,* vol. 9, no. 4 (July/August), p. 3; *The Truth About the Homosexual,* 1–2.

16. Marian Wallace, *"Junior Scholastic* Pushes Gay Agenda," *Family Voice,* vol. 15, no. 5 (May 1993), p. 29.

17. Anonymous response to Robert Dawidoff. In possession of authors.

18. Robertson, op. cit., pp. 116–17.

19. Sara Diamond, *Spiritual Warfare* (Boston: South End Press, 1989), pp. 33–34; Mario Cuomo quoted in Wills, op. cit., p. 311.

20. *The Advocate,* April 7, 1992, p. 27.

21. Peter Gomes, "Homophobic? Reread Your Bible," *The New York Times,* August 17, 1992, p. A18; John Boswell, *Christianity, Social Tolerance and Homosexuality* (Chicago: University of Chicago Press, 1980), p. 100.

22. Gomes, op. cit.

23. *The Reformer,* vol. 9, no. 4 (July/August 1993), p. 3.

24. Matthew 10: 14–15.

25. Boswell, op. cit., pp. 6–7.

26. H. Shelton Smith, *In His Image But* . . . (Durham, N.C.: Duke University Press, 1972), p. 129.

27. Baptist Convention quoted in *The Advocate,* April 7, 1992, p. 20; English Society of Friends quoted in *Homosexuality and Ethics* (New York: Pilgrim Press, 1981), p. 137.

28. Reverend Mel White quoted in *Los Angeles Times,* July 26, 1993, p. E6.

Chapter 5: The Ghost in the Machine
1. Alfred Kinsey, *Sexual Behavior in the Human Male* (Philadelphia: W. B. Saunders, 1948), p. 650; Kinsey, *Sexual Behavior in the Human Female* (Philadelphia: W. B. Saunders, 1953), p. 488.

2. Adrienne Rich, "Compulsory Heterosexuality and Lesbian Experience," *Signs: A Journal of Women in Culture and Society,* vol. 5, no. 4, p. 651.

3. *The Advocate,* April 7, 1992, p. 27.

4. *The Advocate,* September 19, 1992, p. 19. The August 1, 1992, *Proceedings of the National Academy of Sciences* reported that, based on a comparative study of the brains of gay men with heterosexual men and women, sexual differences in the brain affect not only brain structure but also behavior. Earlier in 1992, Dr. Simon Le Vay of the Salk Institute reported that a region of the hypothalamus—an area of the brain that helps regulate sexual behavior—is smaller in gay men than in heterosexual men. These preliminary findings remain inconclusive and controversial. For example, see commentaries by Ruth Hubbard and by Chandler Burr, *The New York Times,* August 2, 1993.

5. See John D'Emilio, *Sexual Politics, Sexual Communities* (Chicago: University of Chicago Press, 1983), pp. 58–74; Stuart Timmons, *The Trouble with Harry Hay* (Boston: Alyson, 1990), pp. 139–71.

6. *USA Today,* March 30, 1992.

7. *Bowers v. Hardwick* (1986), 478 US 186; *Materson v. Marchello* (A.D. 2d Dept. 1984) 473 NYS2d 998, 1005. The plaintiff sued the defendants for defamation because they had referred to his "boyfriend." The defendants argued that the statement was not defamatory because homosexuality no longer carried a social stigma. The court rejected the argument, observing that "despite the fact that an increasing number of homosexuals are publicly expressing satisfaction and even pride in their status, a false charge of homosexuality cannot be ignored."

8. *The Advocate,* April 7, 1992, p. 27.

9. Hannah Arendt, *The Jew as Pariah* (New York: Grove Press, 1978), p. 121.

10. George Bush on having a gay grandchild. *The New York Times,* August 12, 1992, section 1, p. 1.

11. Thomas A. Stewart, "Gay in Corporate America," *Fortune,* December 16, 1991, p. 44.

12. *Olmstead v. United States* (1928) 277 U.S. 438, 478 (Brandeis, J., dissenting).

Chapter 6: What Do They Want, Anyway?

1. David Mixner on NBC.

2. *USA Today*, August 25, 1992.

3. John Boswell, *Christianity, Social Tolerance and Homosexuality* (Chicago: University of Chicago Press, 1980), p. 82.

4. Alissa Friedman, *"The Necessity for State Recognition of Same-Sex Marriage:* Constitutional Requirements and Evolving Notions of Family," 3 *Berkeley Women's Law Journal* (1988), pp. 134–70.

5. *Alvany v. Powell* (1854), 54 N.C. (1 Jones Esq.) 35, quoted in Karen A. Gutman, "Sexual Control in the Slaveholding South," *Harvard Women's Law Journal* (1984) pp. 7, 115, 116, n. 7. Virginia code sections 20–57, 20–59, quoted in *Loving v. Virginia* (1966) 388 U.S. 1, 4; *Baehr v. Lewin* (Hawaii, 1993) 852 P.2d 44, 62.

6. William G. Axinn and Arland Thornton, "The Relationship Between Cohabitation and Divorce Selectivity or Casual Influence," *Demography* 29 (August 1992)3:357, 361.

7. For legal definition of marriage in California, California West Codes Annotated, Civil Code Section 4100.

8. *Singer v. Hara* (1974), 522 P.2d 1187, 1191.

9. Mary Mendola, *The Mendola Report: A New Look at Gay Couples* (1980), p. 254.

10. See for example studies published in Fredrick W. Bozett, ed., *Gay and Lesbian Parents* (New York: Praeger, 1987), pp. 39–137 and, Fredrick W. Bozett and Marvin B. Sussman, eds., *Homosexuality and Family Relations* (New York: The Howorth Press, 1990).

11. Steven Mintz, "Regulating the American Family," *Journal of Family History*, 14 (Oct. 1989) 4:405; David Stannard "Changes in the American Family: Fiction or Reality," pp. 83–96 from Virginia Tufte and Barbara Myeroff, eds. *Changes Images of the Family* (New Haven: Yale Univ. Press, 1979). Also see Stephanie Coontz, *The Social Origins of Private Life: A History of American Families, 1600–1900* (London: Verso, 1988); see Chapter 9, "Results and Prospects: Towards the Twentieth-Century Family"; see especially pp. 330–339.

12. *Baehr v. Lewin,* supra, 852 P.2d at 58, 58, 59.

13. Ibid., 59, 63.

14. Ibid., 68.

SATAN IS THE FATHER OF ALL LIARS!!! GOD IS PUNISHING EVERYONE WHO VOTED FOR CLINTON!

Clinton jumps into trap of gay-haters

By ROBERT DAWIDOFF

President Clinton's answer to a minister's recent question about gays and lesbians in the military was correctly taken as a retreat from his original stated intention to issue an executive order banning discrimination against homosexual soldiers. The president said "most Americans believe that the gay lifestyle should not be promoted by the military or anybody else in this country." And, he added, he seeks a compromise that "does not appear to endorse a gay lifestyle."

This phrase, "gay lifestyle," has become the key code word of anti-gay activists. For this president to have employed it, especially in a public answer to a question about homosexuals in the military, signals more than a move away from another one of his public positions. It is a changing of sides on a significant civil-rights issue.

Central to the anti-gay position is the notion that sexual orientation is not an immutable characteristic requiring equal protection of the laws, but a matter of choice. It is easier to persist in anti-homosexual prejudice if you believe that homosexuality is like adultery, something you choose to do, rather than, like heterosexuality, something you are. **WORSE**

Scientists have only begun to investigate this subject, although recent studies of brain chemistry and of the incidence of lesbian and gay twins suggest that sexual orientation is genetically inherent. Few reputable scientists credit the notion that homosexuals can choose their sexual orientation. Even if sexual orientation results from what some social scientists call "cultural formation," it still presents itself to most lesbian and gay people as a fact rather than a choice.

Talking about a gay "lifestyle" is a rhetorical device by which anti-gay activists can associate the ordinary lives that gay and lesbian Americans lead with habits and practices that they know will incite other ordinary Americans against us. What homosexual Americans do choose to do, in ever-increasing numbers, is to "come out" and press their claim for equal protection of the laws. This is the real choice that has stirred up controversy.

Early in his election campaign, Clinton told gay and lesbian groups that they were a part of his encompassing vision and promised executive action to reverse prejudice. Michael Dukakis in 1988 refused organized gay money because he knew that if elected, he could not make good on any promises he

SODOM AND GOMORRAH DESTROYED — FAST — HOLY BIBLE

might make to the community. Clinton asked for and got our support because he said he believed in our civil rights. And now he is telling the people for whom the promise of gay rights is a threat to their religiously established moral order that nobody is going to promote the "gay lifestyle."

Maybe one of the various compromises under discussion will end the anti-gay witch-hunting in the military. Maybe not. But one thing is certain: With or without the president, homosexual Americans are embarked on a civil-rights movement. **GOING NOWHERE!** Civil-rights movements have historically been necessary because the prejudice that sustains discrimination is widespread and serves powerful interests. Partly for that reason, presidents have generally been followers, not leaders, in civil rights. Even so, the words that President Clinton chose are ominous for Americans who recognize that what is at stake here is not lifestyle but life, as in life, liberty and the pursuit of happiness. **No Civil Rights For Perverts who Spread AIDS.**

□ *Robert Dawidoff is a professor of history at Claremont Graduate School and the author, with Michael Nava, of "Created Equal: Why Gay Rights Matter to America," to be published next year. He wrote this article for the Los Angeles Times.*

A response to an article Robert Dawidoff wrote for the
L.A. Times, sent anonymously to the author.